More Praise for *Stepping Up*, Se

"*Stepping Up* is not a lecture but an
that will help your personal life, help
business, and help change the world.   ....ows
how, by taking responsibility for the m.,_. ....c.as of our lives—family,
work, community—we release tremendous energy and creativity to
work for positive change."

—**Duane Elgin, author of *Voluntary Simplicity* and *The Living Universe***

"This book compels us all to step up and draw on our courage to help
realize positive change—either within our immediate circle of influence or in a wide-reaching manner. Once again, Dr. Izzo's research,
unparalleled storytelling, and actionable advice present a gift that
can significantly enrich our personal and professional lives."

—**Josh Blair, Executive Vice President, Human Resources, TELUS**

"The fastest ticket to success in career and life is to do something
worth doing! That won't happen if you play it safe, point fingers at
others, or act like a victim. As a senior HR executive, I have always
found that you have to take a stand to make a difference. *Stepping
Up* is filled with stories of people who stepped up, spoke up, took initiative, and made their companies (and the world) better. If you want
to get ahead in your career, then read this book and follow its advice."

—**Brigid Pelino, Senior Vice President, Human Resources, Economical
Insurance**

"*Stepping Up* is an insightful and timely read. John Izzo has delicately
woven inspirational stories with practical examples of how any leader
who chooses to step up and make a difference can truly make the
world a better place."

—**Ferio Pugliese, Senior Vice President, Government Relations, Air
Canada**

"*Stepping Up* is an empowering, immensely freeing book based on an
exquisitely simple concept. Izzo combines evidence-based insights
with action-provoking stories of hope, reminding us of the game-
changing power that quietly lies within reach of every person."

—**Susan Biali, MD, author of *Live a Life You Love***

"John Izzo's *Stepping Up* is a remarkable book. It shows how each of us can do what needs doing, no matter how big and intractable the problem. Reading it is sure to propel anyone into meaningful action."
—**Mark Levy, founder of Levy Innovation and author of** ***Accidental Genius***

"John Izzo has 'stepped up' in writing this book to engage all of us in making the world a better place. It begins with a very simple premise: we must each take responsibility for the fixing. Izzo understands the concept of scale and shows us, through stories, the many levels of influence each one of us has access to. Doing our part, at whatever level we can, makes the world a better place even as it makes us feel empowered and enriched. This is a guidebook for making a difference written by a wonderful guide."
—**Joel Barker, futurist, filmmaker, and author**

"*Stepping Up* makes a timely and important contribution to leadership thinking and practice. Dr. Izzo shows how all of us are capable of stepping up and making a difference in our work and personal lives. This book is a must-read for all managers and supervisors."
—**Bob Peter, Former President and CEO, LCBO**

Stepping
Up

Other books by this author

Awakening Corporate Soul (with Eric Klein)

Second Innocence

The Five Secrets You Must Discover Before You Die

The Five Thieves of Happiness

The Purpose Revolution (with Jeff Vanderwielen)

Stepping Up

How Taking Responsibility Changes Everything

Second Edition

JOHN IZZO, PhD

BK

Berrett–Koehler Publishers, Inc.

Copyright © 2011, 2020 by John B. Izzo
All rights reserved. No part of this publication may be reproduced, distributed, or transmitted in any form or by any means, including photocopying, recording, or other electronic or mechanical methods, without the prior written permission of the publisher, except in the case of brief quotations embodied in critical reviews and certain other noncommercial uses permitted by copyright law. For permission requests, write to the publisher, addressed "Attention: Permissions Coordinator," at the address below.

Berrett-Koehler Publishers, Inc.
1333 Broadway, Suite 1000
Oakland, CA 94612-1921
Tel: (510) 817-2277   Fax: (510) 817-2278   www.bkconnection.com

ORDERING INFORMATION
Quantity sales. Special discounts are available on quantity purchases by corporations, associations, and others. For details, contact the "Special Sales Department" at the Berrett-Koehler address above.
Individual sales. Berrett-Koehler publications are available through most bookstores. They can also be ordered directly from Berrett-Koehler:
Tel: (800) 929-2929; Fax: (802) 864-7626; www.bkconnection.com.
Orders for college textbook / course adoption use.
Please contact Berrett-Koehler: Tel: (800) 929-2929; Fax: (802) 864-7626.

Distributed to the US trade and internationally by Penguin Random House Publisher Services.

Berrett-Koehler and the BK logo are registered trademarks of Berrett-Koehler Publishers, Inc.

Printed in the United States of America

Berrett-Koehler books are printed on long-lasting acid-free paper. When it is available, we choose paper that has been manufactured by environmentally responsible processes. These may include using trees grown in sustainable forests, incorporating recycled paper, minimizing chlorine in bleaching, or recycling the energy produced at the paper mill.

Library of Congress Cataloging-in-Publication Data
Names: Izzo, John B. (John Baptist), 1957- author.
Title: Stepping up : how taking responsibility changes everything / John Izzo, Ph.D.
Description: Second edition. | Oakland, CA : Berrett-Koehler Publishers, [2020] | Includes index.
Identifiers: LCCN 2020033728 | ISBN 9781523091454 (paperback ; alk. paper) | ISBN 9781523091461 (adobe pdf) | ISBN 9781523091478 (epub)
Subjects: LCSH: Responsibility. | Organizational behavior. | Organizational change. | Social change. | Leadership.
Classification: LCC BJ1451 .I99 2020 | DDC 179/.9--dc23
LC record available at https://lccn.loc.gov/2020033728

SECOND EDITION
26 25 24 23 22 21 20   10 9 8 7 6 5 4 3 2 1

Interior design: Adriane Bosworth
Cover design: Karen Marquardt

To my mother—Irene Parisi Izzo.
In your own quiet way you stepped up
for what was right and I continue to live in
the light of your moon even in your absence.

Contents

Foreword

John Izzo's *Stepping Up* is one of those books with a strong message that can benefit everyone who is open to it. John's message, "Stepping up is seeing a need and deciding YOU are the right person to do something about it," hits home at a time when the world needs people to do just that—step UP!

I work with organizations every day, and what I find is that very often there isn't a lot of stepping up during or after a crisis. There is a lot of finger-pointing, blaming others, and passing the buck. It's the CEO's fault; it's a team member's fault; it's the boss's fault. After a crisis at home, the same rule applies. Blame it on the spouse, the dog, the kids, the sprinklers. Very few people point the finger of responsibility at themselves. People are more inclined to pass the buck than they are to take responsibility.

The fact is, though, passing the buck doesn't build your character or give you the opportunity to learn from your mistakes. In a nutshell, it doesn't make you rich. This behavioral flaw is as significant a negative attribute as the positive qualities of brainpower, courage, and resourcefulness. A leader who cannot shoulder the blame is not someone people will follow or trust. They will, however, question the leader's character, dependability, and loyalty, and they will hold back their loyalty from him or her.

You know people who accept responsibility—aren't they great to be around? These people do things like help more and judge less. They try to get people to focus on a future they can influence, not a past they cannot change. They help others take responsibility for their own behavior. They reflect on past events and ask, "What can we learn from that?" They don't, and they encourage others not to, speak when angry or out of control. And they think before they speak, asking themselves, "Will this comment help?"

In this book you will read about many people and groups who do all of these things, how they navigate taking responsibility and grow a culture where this is the norm. You can also learn to be more like them if you're not already. *Stepping Up* is a wonderful testament to those individuals and teams who do step up! I encourage you to read it and enjoy it—and if you change a little bit because of it, that is OK too.

Life is good.

Marshall Goldsmith

Executive coach and author
of the *New York Times* bestsellers
MOJO and *What Got You Here
Won't Get You There*

Preface to the Second Edition

It has been almost a decade now since I first wrote *Stepping Up*. The idea was simple, but I hoped profound, that taking responsibility changes EVERYTHING! Over this past decade I have given over five hundred keynote speeches on *Stepping Up*, and my team has conducted several thousand workshops challenging people to step up to see the power of personal responsibility in life and work.

Although I have authored or coauthored a total of eight books, this is the first time I made the choice to write a second edition of a book. So I thought it would be valuable to tell you why I made that choice as well as the changes I chose to make.

It seems to me that there are only two reasons to publish a new edition of a book. First, because the book and its ideas are having a real impact on readers and those exposed to the ideas and new examples can extend the life of that impact. Second, because the author has something new to add that was not available when the book was written. These were the two reasons I took the time to create this second edition.

The book and the ideas presented in it have proven to be of great value to both individuals and the organizations that have adopted its principles. Hundreds of organizations are now using the ideas from the book, and some of them, like Qantas Airlines, have put thousands of people through training experiences to shift them to stepping up to 100 percent responsibility. I have witnessed personally the profound shift that occurs when people choose to see themselves as agents of change and when organizations create a climate for stepping up.

While there are many examples that come to mind, let me illustrate two—one personal and one organizational. About two years after the book was published, I was doing a series of leadership speaking events for Northrop Grumman, the aerospace company. Leaders were given copies of the book to read ahead of our sessions. At one of the sessions a woman in her forties told me that she had to apologize for not reading the book. Her sixteen-year-old son had seen the book lying around and started reading it. She went on to tell me he loved it so much he had refused to surrender it until he was finished. She then said, "I've seen a huge positive shift in him over the last few weeks."

The second story is what happened when we put almost twenty thousand team members at Qantas Airlines through a program on stepping up over a several-year period. Over that period, we got to witness a shift in the culture of an entire organization toward focusing on what each person can do to make things better. People went from pointing the finger out at others to looking in the mirror. The then CEO of the domestic airline division, Lyell Strambi, said "For the first time, when we went through a crisis it felt like we were on the same side."

This mirrors the hundreds of companies around the world that are using the 100/0 Principle that is featured in the book. Most months I get emails from companies all over the world that have adopted this simple idea with profound impact.

My first motivation for a new edition was to update the book with new examples of people who stepped up and to update those from the first edition. I hope this will bring a fresh coat of paint to what have turned out to be enduring ideas.

The second reason to do a new edition is because there is something new to be said. Since the time I wrote the book a decade ago, my colleagues and I have had the opportunity to learn a great deal of what it means to step up. People often ask us, How do I know when I am stepping up?

So one of the big additions is a new chapter titled "Stepping Up or Stepping Back—How to Know the Difference." Since the first edition we have identified five behavioral markers to know when we are stepping up. This new chapter makes clear what it means to step up and what it means to step back. It helps each of us decide, moment to moment, what it means to be in a place of 100 percent responsibility.

I have also added two self-assessments. The first helps us assess whether we are in a place of self-responsibility personally, and the second helps leaders assess whether we are creating a culture conducive to responsibility in our organization or team. Both of these tools have proven to be valuable to our clients.

Finally, I am even more convinced now than I was in 2010 about the crying need for personal responsibility in society and the power of it in our personal lives. In my talks and workshops around the globe, I often ask people this binary question: "Over the last decade, do you think we have become more of a society of 'innies' and personal responsibility or a society of 'outies' where we mostly blame others and the outside world for our circumstances?" I ask for a show of hands. Across the many countries and types of audiences I speak to, about 90 percent of hands vote for a shift away from personal responsibility. The need for this book and its core ideas is greater than ever. Now more than ever, we need to take 100 percent responsibility to solve the challenges of our time and pursue the opportunities in our own lives.

Preface to the First Edition

This book is for people who want to make a bigger difference in their community, organization, or the world. It is for anyone who wants a better marriage or to improve career prospects. It is a book for all leaders or business owners who would like to help their people act more like owners. It is a book for anyone who believes in, or wants to believe in, the power of individuals to create change.

I began writing this book when I was ten years old. At the time, my television set was filled with images of people stepping up. All over the world, people were taking great personal risks to make the world a better place: African Americans withstood fire hoses in the streets of the South, peace activists sounded a warning call about the nuclear arms race, dissidents spoke out in totalitarian regimes, and women asserted their rights as equal citizens. I decided I wanted to become a journalist so I could tell the stories of those who made things better.

In my smaller personal world I listened with rapt attention to the sermons of the Reverend Robert Kelly at Calvary Presbyterian Church in New York City, challenging each of us to do what we could to combat racism and the ills of our day.

"The world is waiting for us to step up," he admonished us. He noted that the need lay not just in the large issues of the day but in the "smaller world in which we live every day, where we can make a large difference in the lives of others."

The stories of those who step up and make things better have always fascinated me. As human beings, we learn through stories, and it has been that way for thousands of years. We remember the stories long after we forget the lectures, which is why my life has been devoted to telling stories. In my books on corporate culture I tell the stories of great companies and leaders who inspired passion at work. In my book and television series *The Five Secrets You Must Discover Before You Die* I tell the stories of two hundred fifty people from age 60 to 106 who had been identified as having found true happiness. Through their stories I hoped to show the path to lasting fulfillment.

After I finished that book, which became a bestseller and was translated into over a dozen languages, it seemed to me that another story had yet to be told. Why do some people step up and make a bigger difference than others? What role does taking personal responsibility play in creating happiness and creating change? How can the stories of those who step up inform each of us about solving the great issues of our day, whether the issue is making better families, stopping bullying, making our marriages better, improving a company, or tackling the many societal issues we face?

It occurred to me that each case comes down to responsibility. The definition for stepping up in this book is simple: *Stepping up is seeing a need and deciding you are the right person to do something about it.* It is about doing what you can in your sphere of influence to create change, not looking to anyone else. The responsibility I speak of is not a wagging finger telling you to step up, but an empowering message of what happens when we stop worrying about what anyone else is doing and choose to do what we can do. Whether trying to change our family, our company, or the world, we are powerful only when we focus on what *we* can do.

Because I believe we learn best through stories, my research for this book involved finding stories of people who had stepped up and created change. I did not want to tell stories we have all heard before nor find famous people to hear their tales. Instead, I set out to find stories that few of us know about that illustrate the incredible power to create change when we decide to act in our sphere of influence. I tried to find people whose stories of taking action were broad and instructive, rather than seek a scientific random sample of people who had stepped up. The stories range from a homeless man who started a recycling revolution and a shopkeeper in Italy who stood up to the Mafia to a group of nurses and housekeepers who helped transform the image of their hospital and a woman who turned a dying business into a profit center. Some were trying to save the world, some were trying to grow or improve their business, others just wanted to have a positive influence on the people around them, and some wanted better relationships.

The book has two main thrusts: the value of taking responsibility and how to step up. The first three chapters make the case for why taking responsibility matters. My intention is not to lecture you but to show how our lives, careers, relationships, organizations, and communities will be radically better if we start looking to ourselves to change things and stop looking to (or pointing at) someone else. The principle is simple but profound. When we decide to do what we can, where we are, instead of looking for others to do it, we feel more powerful and accomplish more. What's more, beyond our personal world most of the great problems of our day can be solved only by each of us deciding to take action in our sphere of power.

The second thrust of the book identifies the keys to stepping up and having more influence. Through the inspiring stories of individuals who stepped up to make things better,

I hope to show you that stepping up is neither a great mystery nor reserved for a chosen few. By following the example of these people, we too can step up and make a difference in our relationships, our companies, and our communities. Finally, I show how we can create a culture for stepping up in a company, family, or society. At the end of each chapter, I offer practical ways for each of us to step up and take responsibility starting right now.

Unless otherwise noted the stories in this book come from personal interviews with the people whose stories I tell. At the end of the book I have a list of some resources to help you connect with others who are stepping up.

For me, this is more than a book; I hope it is part of a movement. Now more than ever we need people to step up. We need each of us to stop pointing out and start looking inside instead. My hope is that by telling these stories, the book will inspire you to tell your story.

CHAPTER 1

The Five Rows of Responsibility

Each of us influences only about five rows, but in
that sphere of influence the world is changed.

Responsibility changes everything. The moment we decide
that we are the ones who are capable of and responsible for
changing things everything shifts. This is a book about how
your marriage, your career, your life, your company, and our
world gets better whenever one of us simply decides to step up
and do what we can do in our sphere of influence.

Seeing ourselves as responsible and powerful to change
things is a game changer in the deepest sense. The shift is
akin to the childhood game of tag. When I was a child in
New York City, we played endless hours of this game. One
person was *It* and had to run around trying to tag someone
else. The moment you were tagged, the whole game changed.

Well, you are It! You are responsible for your own happiness, for the success of your relationships, for the morale of
your workplace, for the success of the company where you
work, and for your life. What's more, you are responsible for
poverty, for global warming, for your neighborhood, for your
school, and for homelessness. Better said, we are all It. That is,
when each of us takes responsibility, stepping up to do what
we can, everything gets better. Not only that, but when we step

up and take responsibility, the game of life and work is more fun and more rewarding. We find more success.

This is not to say that there aren't times when our lives, our happiness, and our success are significantly influenced by outside forces. Sometimes our manager is a tyrant, sometimes parents aren't able to give us a good foundation, sometimes our spouse is more to blame than we are, and sometimes the problems we face (such as global warming) seem so intractable that it is easy to feel like we can't make a difference. But when we choose to focus on what *we* can do and how *we* can act, we are suddenly powerful. Victims simply don't create change.

I am not talking about "the burden of responsibility." Many of us already feel too responsible, taking on the blame and feeling a need to fix everything. The responsibility I refer to is freeing. It is about choosing to do what you can in your sphere of influence without worrying about what anyone else is or is not doing.

The Five Rows of Responsibility

One of the simplest yet most profound experiences of my life happened to me on an airplane almost twenty years ago. It was an icy, snowy day in Cleveland, and I arrived just in time to be the last one on the plane before they closed the door. I quickly realized that everyone around me was in a foul mood. No sooner had I sat down than the stranger next to me said, "My boss is such an idiot! He is sending me up here to this godforsaken place. The client never buys anything and never will buy anything. My boss is such an idiot." Having overheard her diatribe, the man across the aisle chimed in with his own commentary: "Not only is your boss an idiot, lady, but the people who run this airline are idiots too. We have no leg room, we are late as always, and look at the ice on these wings—we're probably going to die on this thing."

Once we took off, the mood continued, and the negative virus spread. Soon everyone around me was complaining about the world, their companies, and their spouses, and it just kept getting worse. Even I was calling my boss an idiot, and I work for myself! It was a veritable feast of negativity and victim thinking. Like all feasts of junk food, the feast felt good going down but left all of us feeling worse.

About five rows in front of me at the bulkhead a mother sat with her two-year-old son. All through the first half hour of the flight, the kid kept trying without success to get his head above the seat to look back. A few times I saw his head, another time his eyebrows, but it was not until about forty minutes into the flight that he finally got his head above the seat and rested his chin and hands on the seat. He looked something like a chipmunk.

When he saw all of the passengers behind him, he smiled the biggest, most natural smile you've ever seen. Within moments that child transformed the five rows behind him. The boss-is-an-idiot lady started talking to me about her kids. The airline-is-run-by-idiots guy stopped complaining and began making faces as he tried to get the boy to smile again. Someone said, "We should all be a little more positive like that kid," and suggested I go borrow him. When I offered to take the child off the mother's hands for a little bit, his mother gladly accepted the break, and the boy's visit to row six changed the mood within minutes.

Sitting there at thirty thousand feet rattling across the Midwest, I had an epiphany that I have come to call *The Five Rows Principle:* most of us have tremendous power to influence about five rows around us, but we spend most of our time thinking about and talking about what someone else should do in some other plane or row. What's more, almost every problem we face—from global warming and terrorism to poor morale in a business and bullying in schools—is a five rows problem. That is, the problem is merely the aggregate of what each of us is doing in our five rows.

Let's take an example of a seemingly intractable problem. Why is global warming and a deteriorating environment such a vexing problem? Because the environment, like most problems, is a five rows problem. You could say the government needs to step up, but the problem is the aggregate result of decisions each one of us (and our companies) makes in our five rows—the cars we drive, the trips we take or don't take, the food we eat, the choices we make in terms of what we buy, what we reuse or recycle, and so on. On one hand our five rows don't matter very much at all, but on the other hand the problem will be solved only when each of us does what we can in our five rows.

Take a company where bad service and low morale have become the norm. You could say that the CEO needs to fix it, but soon you would realize that for the most part service and morale are both five rows problems. Things will change only when individuals step up in their five rows and treat the customer better or do their part to improve morale. What's more, individuals need to focus on what *they* can do in their five rows instead of what someone else should do. The CEO should be worried about what she can do in her sphere, the managers in theirs, and the frontline people in their sphere. The more people focus on taking action themselves, the more likely we are to make progress. If we focus on our five rows, we can create change. We can't control what anyone else does, only what we do.

This conclusion applies as easily to our personal lives as to these larger landscapes. Reeling from a quarrel with my wife that day on my ride to the airport, I was focused on what my wife needed to do to fix our marriage instead of taking responsibility for my "five rows." The more I focused on what she should do, the less powerful I felt, and the less impact I could have. Whether it is in our personal or our communal life, we must always begin by asking what we can do, not what others should do.

If we all begin in our five rows, every problem we face can be fixed. Every challenge we have can be solved. Every time you are tempted to think it does not matter if you step up, remember the five rows principle: if each of us begins where we are and does what we can, anything is possible. Pointing to someone else is easy and ultimately means no one does anything.

Stepping Up: Claiming Our Power to Change Things

The good news is that every day some people decide they can, must, and will change things. I call this *stepping up*. It is the simple act of seeing a need and deciding that you are the right person to do something about it.

That is exactly what happened in 1992 when two young teachers, Dave Levin and Mike Feinberg, began their teaching careers in Houston, Texas, through Teach for America, an innovative program established in 1990 to place top college graduates as teachers in high-need public schools. Teach for America is an organization that was founded by Wendy Kopp, an example of someone who stepped up. Her undergraduate thesis at Princeton convinced her that an elite corps of teachers would draw many of the best and brightest of her generation to teach in low-income communities. As a twenty-one-year-old, she raised $2.5 million and started with a corps of five hundred teachers in 1990. Today, Teach for America has a corps of over twenty-eight thousand teachers. Wendy has written a book, *A Chance to Make History* (Public Affairs, 2010), which details some of the lessons learned from Teach for America.

Mike and Dave left the program in the fall of 1992 and their first assignment was at two inner city elementary schools with poor records of academic success. The first months were hard, and by midyear their classes were, by their own description, a disaster. While they were failing miserably with the kids, a teacher named Harriett had a classroom just down the hall filled with enthusiastic students chanting, having fun, and learning. *Maybe it was not the kids; maybe it was the teacher.* Recognizing that situation was Mike and Dave's first act of responsibility.

They befriended Harriett, and she became their mentor. The young teachers learned how to reach even the most difficult kids. By the end of the year, their classrooms were lively and engaged. The year ended on a high note, with students doing homework and performing well. The youngsters proceeded enthusiastically to middle school.

"We naïvely thought we had done it. In one school year we had reformed education," Mike told me.

Then reality set in. The next term, the students who had gone off to middle school started calling Dave and Mike saying things like, "They don't give us any homework, and we can't take the books home." By midyear, their former students— kids they were sure they had prepared for life and success— had joined the chorus line of underperformers smoking dope, playing hooky, and joining gangs.

When they first realized the outcome of their good work, Dave and Mike went into a several-month funk. They found themselves sitting alongside others in the teachers lounge pointing outward.

"We pointed fingers at everyone," Mike said. "We blamed the district, the superintendent, the parents, the community, and even society itself. We had done our job, and everyone else had failed these kids."

Then one night in 1993 Mike and Dave had their road to Damascus, a Jerry McGuire–like moment of clarity.

"That night, we suddenly stopped pointing the finger out and instead pointed the finger at ourselves," Mike said. "We looked in the mirror instead of the magnifying glass. We realized that *we* were the ones who had failed. Whatever we had done as teachers was not enough to prepare them to succeed after they left our class. We asked the question, How could we prepare them for middle school, high school, college, and life? What could we do as teachers that would form a foundation that could not be broken?"

The pair put U2's *Achtung Baby* CD on repeat, and by 5:00 a.m. they had outlined an educational revolution called KIPP (Knowledge Is Power Program) on their computer screen. The idea was simple and profound. Start earlier, end later, hold classes every other Saturday morning, give two to three hours of homework every night, and ask the parents, teachers, and students to take personal responsibility by making commitments.

"It was a very spiritual night," Mike told me. "That night, we realized that if we stepped up we could change things."

He said, "The basic principle was simple. If we committed ourselves to becoming truly great teachers, to increase the amount of time we were willing to teach the kids, then it was possible to prepare them for success in college and in life. We did not have to revamp the system; we just had to work hard to become better teachers, thus motivating kids to stay longer."

They went to the principal at Garcia Elementary in Houston and found a receptive audience. When it came time to get approval from the district, however, the answer was initially no.

"They asked us if we were changing the curriculum, and we said no," Mike said. "We told them smart people have created the curriculum. They said, 'How can it be educational reform if you are not creating new curriculum?' Then we said, 'The kids will start at 7:30 a.m. and end at 5:00 p.m.' So they said, 'So you want to do an early hours and after-school program?' We said, 'No. The kids will start early and end late and come in every other Saturday, but it will be one long school day.' In the end they told us, 'Look, we don't get it, but, if you can find fifty parents and kids crazy enough to do it, we will let you do it.' So Dave and I went door to door like vacuum cleaner salesmen, and when we were done, we had the fifty parents and kids who had said yes."

Years of hard work and many setbacks followed, but the model turned out to be incredibly successful. As of July 2011, KIPP had one hundred and nine schools, sixty-one of them middle schools (grades 5–8), thirty elementary schools (grades pre-K–4), and eighteen high schools (grades 9–12) serving over thirty-two thousand students in twenty states and the District of Columbia. All but one is a charter school within public school systems, and students are accepted regardless of academic record, prior conduct, or socioeconomic background. About one-third of KIPP's teachers and over half of its principals are alumni of Teach for America (www.teachforamerica.org). Over 80 percent of KIPP students are from low-income families, and 95 percent are African American or Latino. Nationally, over 90 percent of KIPP middle school students have gone on to college-preparatory high schools, and over 85 percent of KIPP alumni have gone on to college. These numbers are far above the averages for their respective communities, and the public wants more. In Houston alone, eight thousand students are on a waiting list for twelve-hundred seats.

Most of all, the work of these two teachers and others who followed them has challenged a longstanding paradigm that inner city kids were destined to be defined by demographics.[1]

I asked Mike what it takes to step up and change things. "First you can't be about blaming others," he said. "Our first reaction was to point out. But you can't do anything about what is out there. When you look in the mirror, suddenly you have the power to do something." Not coincidentally, KIPP schools are built on the same simple philosophy that there are no shortcuts. If you work hard, you will achieve. It is a message of self-responsibility in its purest form. If you are not succeeding, look in the mirror.

Such sentiments are enough to craze a person who has a disdain for motivational speakers or inspirational books, but the results are too compelling. The moment we look outside instead of inside, we are like Superman around kryptonite: our power disappears. Even the message at KIPP is right on. They don't say that demographics don't *influence* destiny, only that it does not *determine* destiny. The distinction is subtle but profound. Our community, our parents, our zip code, our upbringing, our height, our looks, and the lucky breaks we get—all of these things *influence* our destiny, but they don't *determine* it. That is why personal responsibility is vitally important. The moment we focus on what we can change instead of what others must do, everything changes.

Malcolm Gladwell takes a look at this concept in his fascinating book, *Outliers*. Although he shows that being in the right place at the right time does significantly influence achievement, he also demonstrates that ten thousand hours of practice will make you an expert in just about anything. My point is that you can't do anything about the right time and the right place, but you *can* do something about yourself, and I believe what you do is ultimately the most important factor in achievement.

The Responsibility Ripple

Have you ever noticed that, when you yawn, it's highly likely someone around you will also yawn? Recently, I yawned, and even my dog yawned! We all know that yawning is contagious, but have you ever wondered why?

After years of trying to answer that question, researchers concluded that the most obvious answer is the correct one: we yawn because imitating the behavior of others is a natural human trait. We yawn together for the same reason that we smile when a stranger smiles at us or that we laugh when someone else laughs at a joke, even if we don't get the joke. We humans are social beings, and fitting in matters to us. This tendency to imitate may have its roots early in our evolution, because the more we mirror the behavior of others the less likely we are to be seen as a threat.

Human behavior is contagious, good and bad. All of us have had the experience of entering a break room and seeing how one person's complaining about how bad things are "around here" leads to everyone else's joining in the whining feast. We have also had the opposite experience, witnessing how the energy shifts when a few people start talking about how to fix things instead of how broken things are.

Responsibility is contagious. I call this the *responsibility ripple*. When someone steps up to change things, others step up and find courage they had not previously found.

The responsibility ripple is an important principle because the moment we choose to act, the potential for a viral response is always there. Often, however, there is a need for one person, or a few, to be the catalyst that encourages others to step up. An example is the story of Jalen Thompson, a seventeen-year-old in O'Fallon, Missouri, who wanted to join protesters following the death of George Floyd in 2020 in Minneapolis. Floyd's death had ignited protests across the globe against racial injustice and police abuse amidst the backdrop of a global pandemic related to COVID-19.

Thompson and his high school friends had never organized a protest, but they believed that there needed to be protests not only in large cities like nearby Saint Louis but in their smaller community. Thompson also felt it was critical to bring people together, not tear them apart, so he not only initiated the plan for a local protest but met with the local police chief and city officials. When the day for the planned protest arrived, over two thousand people joined in, with Thompson at the front arm in arm with the local police chief. More people participated in the protest there than in much larger cities like Los Angeles on the same day. The story went viral. Like the little boy on my plane ride years ago, Thompson had shown others a path forward to a new way of seeing things.

Standing Up to the Mafia in Naples

Another case in point is Silvana Fucito, a shopkeeper in Naples, Italy, who decided to stand up to the Mafia and ignited a firestorm of resistance right in the heart of Mafia territory. Naples is known for its pizza, but what concerned Silvana was *il pizzo*, the Italian term for protection money merchants pay to local Mafia thugs.

Alongside her husband, Silvana ran a wholesale paint store, a family business that had been around almost thirty years. After years of hard work the business had become quite profitable and grown to have ten employees, but along with the growing profits came more-frequent visits from local thugs and requests for ever-increasing sums of money. The payments were common throughout her neighborhood and had become a resented but accepted part of doing business. Thugs manhandled her husband, helped themselves to merchandise, forced business owners to cash checks of dubious origin, and issued demands that kept getting larger. Silvana reached a boiling point and visited the home of the thugs. She confronted them, saying that she could no longer pay, but pay she did.

In September 2002, the apartment building that housed her family paint store was torched. Except for the good fortune of a mother who happened to be awake late at night feeding an infant, the fire might have cost many lives. At first Silvana was outraged about losing the business she had worked hard to build and the fact that twenty families had come so close to perishing. Yet it was the reaction of many of her neighbors that finally spurred Silvana Fucito into stepping up. Instead of blaming the Mafia, many of her neighbors blamed her for speaking up and fighting back. Sadly, this is often the case; when someone steps up, his or her actions so disturb the status quo that bystanders blame the one who steps up for kicking a hornet's nest.

Turns out, the Mafia burned the wrong woman's store.

A few months after the fire, Silvana founded the San Giovanni Anti-Racket Association aimed at getting residents and the government to put an end to intimidation. In the year before the association was founded, residents reported fewer than two hundred cases of extortion to the police but the number grew to over two thousand within a year! "No Pizzo" signs began to appear in the windows of merchants throughout Naples. The

Italian government, inspired and perhaps embarrassed by the courage of ordinary citizens, began to crack down on the Mafia by seizing properties and closing Mafia enterprises. But Silvana and her association made a big dent in the problem.

In a *Time* magazine article in 2005 she was quoted as saying, "Everyone talks about the politicians and the police, but it is first of all up to us, the citizens. If it's a pizzo or muggings or drugs in your neighborhood, it should make you burn with anger. It must always be the citizens first to demand respect for themselves." (You can read about Silvana Fucito in the *Time* article "Taking on the Mob" by Jeff Israely, dated October 2, 2005, and about the movement in a *Financial Times* article, "Naples Fight to Reclaim the Mafia Badlands," by Guy Dinmore, dated September 27, 2010.)

Silvana Fucito acted and inspired others to do the same. Her actions created a ripple effect, prompting others to step up even though some people at first blamed her for the potentially deadly fire. While she still requires round-the-clock protection, her choice to step up when most would have backed down started a ripple that continues to advance.

Her story is not unique. Throughout this book you will see time and again that choosing to act inspires and challenges others to act. Responsibility has ripples.

The Responsibility Ripple in Daily Life

While the responsibility ripple has an impact on large issues such as standing up to thugs and transforming inner city schools, the effect of this principle can be much more personal. Anyone in an intimate relationship has experienced at some point the cycle of blame that occurs when each partner sees the couple's problems as the other person's fault.

Early in my career I did marriage counseling for several years. In those sessions, I noticed an interesting pattern. Almost inevitably during the first appointment, one member of the couple would announce that whatever issues they had were mostly the fault of his or her partner. In fact, only once in all my sessions did someone say, "Before we get started, I want you to know that it's me we need to work on." Yet it almost always became obvious that both people were contributing. Responsibility begins when we own our part, however large we think it may be.

A friend of mine experienced this cycle of blame when his wife blamed him for her lack of personal time, saying that if he would step up and take more responsibility around the house then she could have more time for herself. From his perspective, she took on duties that did not need to be done and she needed to get their teenage children to take more responsibility. He also felt that part of her enjoyed playing the martyr and that she focused on the family even when she had free time. The two were locked in a turf war with each one blaming the other.

I suggested to him that the situation might shift if he took responsibility for his part. "Maybe she does take on duties that are not necessary," I told him. "Perhaps the kids do need to take more on for themselves. Maybe part of her does want to play the martyr, but you can't do anything about that." I advised him to step up and take responsibility for whatever part of the problem he thought was his. He did just that, telling his wife that she was right, that he had let her take on too much, and that he needed to step up and do more. He began taking on more duties, helping around the house, and taking on more responsibility with their teenage children.

An amazing thing happened. A few weeks later she said to him, "You know, I know that some of this is my doing too.

You are probably right that the kids have learned to count on me for everything. Maybe I need to do what I need to do for myself and trust others to step up."

Now don't get me wrong; marital bliss did not immediately follow, but the energy suddenly shifted from who was to blame to who could do what to fix things. But someone had to take responsibility first. Responsibility created ripples.

Here is another example. My partner, a teacher, had a run-in with a fellow teacher. Her colleague decided to escalate the situation and asked the school principal to intervene and facilitate a conversation about the incident. My partner was furious, as she felt her colleague was entirely at fault, had blown the situation out of proportion, and now had violated an unwritten rule among teachers by not dealing with her directly.

The night before she was going into the facilitated meeting with her fellow teacher, she told me how she was going to "let her have it" and show her how it was all her fault. I suggested that perhaps she might have had some small part in creating the problem. Through discussion, she began to realize that in some small but important ways she too had escalated the situation. The next day, she began the meeting by apologizing for some things she had done that aggravated the problem and said she was even more sorry that her colleague had felt she'd been insensitive. Not surprisingly, that act of taking some responsibility opened up the possibility for her colleague to look at herself. The meeting wound up being productive instead of confrontational.

In every situation, we bear some of the responsibility. When we focus on our part instead of other people's part, something shifts. This simple idea is one of the greatest lessons we can give our children: focus on how you are contributing to any problem instead of what someone else is doing. Take responsibility, and most of the time someone else will take responsibility in return.

The Fascinating Study of Lights in the Theatre

A friend of mine told me about a fascinating study he had read about in university. Researchers filled a movie theatre with participants and projected a small light on the front wall. The study participants were told to raise their hand any time they saw the light move. Several confederates—that is, research team members posing as participants—also sat in the theatre.

After about ten minutes one confederate raised his hand indicating that he had seen the light move. A minute later, another confederate raised his hand. Soon, large numbers of participants also raised their hands to say they had seen the light move. By the end of the study, most participants had said the light had moved, even though the light never moved.

Our human tendency to follow the behavior of others is deeply engrained, as illustrated in that study. This tendency has negative consequences when groups of people act together as a riotous mob. But this trait also means that when we choose to step up to create positive change chances are very good that we will start a chain whose end we cannot ascertain.

Ways to Step Up

✔ **Catch yourself blaming someone for a problem.** When you find yourself in that position, ask yourself, "In what way am I contributing to the problem?" Ask, "What can I do to make things better?"

✔ **Identify your five rows.** Notice who around you might be affected by your actions. If you start smiling more, think how many people around you will be smiling back!

NOTE

1. The KIPP story is not without controversy. Mike Feinberg was let go
   by the board of KIPP in 2018 following a sexual abuse accusation in
   2017. While no criminal charges have been levied to date, the board
   felt there was enough evidence to let him go. Mike has repeatedly
   denied the charges and has retained support among some longtime
   allies in the charter school movement. He's since started a new
   organization called Texas School Venture Fund and worked as a
   consultant at the Center for Education Reform, a Washington, DC–
   based group that supports charters and vouchers.

   Some people have also suggested that organizers have skimmed
   the best students and the most involved parents so that the KIPP
   student group is unique. Thus, the theory goes, such students would
   have thrived in any school, and putting them in a separate program
   may even harm the schools they vacate.

   Still, the KIPP program has inspired many other efforts that have
   produced similar results. Geoffrey Canada, in his book *Whatever It
   Takes*, credits KIPP for influencing what he accomplished in Harlem.
   My own view is that the results speak for themselves. If you want to
   see this in real time, rent the film *Waiting for Superman*.

   People also ask whether KIPP teachers are paid extra for those
   extra hours. Rodrigo Herrera, KIPP's chief people officer, told me,
   "Teacher salaries in many KIPP regions are between 5 and 10 percent
   more than what local districts pay. For recruiting, we notice that the
   great teachers in a traditional district who give their students their
   all are typically already working longer hours. The difference is that
   at KIPP they get paid for that. The reality is that the people we attract
   aren't driven by the salary. We want to pay them enough so they don't
   worry about the money, but they come to us because of the high
   expectations for student achievement and want to work with other
   teachers who share the same perspective."

CHAPTER 2

It's Not My Job,
It's Not My Fault

*There are two kinds of people in the world, those
who make things happen and those who complain
about what's happening.*

How many times in an average week do you hear someone
utter these sentiments? "It's not my job! It was not my fault. It's
just the way I am. It's just the way it is. What can I do about it?
It is bigger than me."

If stepping up is about taking responsibility for change
instead of waiting for others to act, you might ask, "What's in
it for me to step up and take responsibility?" In this chapter,
I make the case that you will be happier and more successful
and ultimately have more influence if you banish such sentiments from your thinking. People who say, "It is my job, some
of it is my doing, I can be different, and I don't accept things
the way they are" are simply happier and more successful than
those who focus outside themselves.

Locus of Control: Are You an Innie
or an Outie?

Locus of control is a concept in social psychology that refers
to how much individuals believe they can control events that
affect them. The concept was first developed by Julian Rotter

in 1954 and has become an important focus in the study of personality. Locus (a Latin word meaning place, location, or situation) can either be internal or external. In the 1960s, Rotter investigated the implications of our tendency to attribute successes and failure either to internal forces (those we have control over) or to external forces (those outside of our influence). We humans fall into one of two camps: Internals, who do things, and Externals, who have things happen to them. Individuals with a high internal locus of control believe that events result primarily from their own behavior and actions. I call these people *innies* or *initiators* because they believe they mostly make their own destiny. Those with an external locus of control believe that powerful others, fate, or chance primarily determine events. These people I call *outies* or *victim thinkers* because they feel that life mostly is done to them rather than through them.

Research shows that external locus of control (victim thinking) is linked to greater stress and a greater tendency toward clinical depression. It has also been linked to poor physical health, anxiety, and learned helplessness. Initiators—people who believe that their actions influence reality—on the other hand, have been shown to be both more successful and happier as well as less prone to social influence.

Organizations are also a lot healthier when filled with people who are initiators rather than victims. Imagine for a moment how people with an external versus an internal locus of control behave within an organization, community, or society. People with an external locus, or victims, will focus on waiting for someone else or something else to determine an organization's destiny. The words *they* and *you* will be the most common start of every sentence. The focus of *they* could be the marketplace, the chief executive, the managers, the competitors, or the economy. People will say, "Things would be better around here if the CEO would do this," "My results would be better if the market would just pick up," and "Service would improve if the other departments would only cooperate." When people talk about their experiences at work, victims will likely see it as someone else's responsibility to make them happy. They will say, "If I had a nicer boss, a better job, if I had gotten that promotion last year, then I'd be happy at work." Victims are also less likely to take initiative because they feel outcomes are not in their hands anyway. An organization filled with victims will generally have low morale, have more risk-averse behavior, and find it difficult to implement change.

People with victim thinking will look at society and say the government should do something about poverty, crime, and the environment. They will throw up their hands at the largest problems we face saying, "What can I, or even we, do about those things?" They may let leaders off the hook, believing that some things simply cannot be fixed because, "It's just the way it is."

Now imagine how an organization or society (or your life) would be different if filled with initiators, people with a strong internal locus of control. When unhappy on their jobs, they would be less likely to blame others and more likely to look inside themselves for answers. If they want to develop their careers, they will ask for what they want instead of complaining that they aren't getting it. Rather than acting like victims, they will take initiative to solve problems. They will probably be less likely to point fingers at the other departments or the marketplace when things go poorly and instead look inside to see how they can change or adapt to the environment. The same can be said within a society. Initiators will be less likely to point the finger at someone else to change things or to hang their head in resignation at the problems we face.

Victim Society?

The truth of course is that most of us sit somewhere between these two extremes. We sometimes act like victims pointing outward, and we sometimes act like initiators looking within. Even those of us who tend to be initiators can act like victims sometimes, and those of us who tend to feel like victims have moments when we see the potential to change things. There are other times when we aren't so much like victims as we simply accept the status quo with a shrug. Victim thinking and scores on locus of control are not identical, but what concerns me is that victim thinking is becoming more pervasive.

After analyzing the results of studies using Rotter's Scale on Locus of Control with young people from 1960 to 2002, Jean Twenge, a prolific researcher at San Diego State University, found a disturbing trend. In a blog post January 26, 2010, on the *Psychology Today* website (www.psychology today.com), Peter Gray reported her findings: "Average scores shifted dramatically . . . for college students—away from the Internal toward the External end of the scale. In fact, the shift was so great that the average young person in 2002 was more external than were 80 percent of young people in the 1960s. The rise in Externality on Rotter's scale over the forty-two-year period showed the same linear trend as did the rise in depression and anxiety."

No wonder *Time* magazine ran a cover story in 2005 with the title "Victim Nation." When I ask audiences in North America if they feel we are becoming more of a society of "innies" or a society of "outies," the show of hands is about 90 percent weighted toward an outward focus. In other words, we feel the shift in our workplaces, schools, and families. Not surprisingly, when LinkedIn conducted a survey of seventeen thousand people across the globe asking what their biggest pet peeves were about colleagues at work, the number one answer, at 78 percent, was "people not taking ownership for their actions" (https://www.huffpost.com/entry /linkedin-survey-top-office-pet-peeves_n_985873).

Some teacher friends of mine tell me about another seismic shift. In a previous generation, if little Johnny was having problems at school, his parents most likely would arrive at the schoolhouse saying, "What is Johnny doing?" Johnny probably got reprimanded by his parents about how he needed to step up. Today, parents are just as likely to come to the school to defend their child, wondering what is wrong with the teachers, the school, and the system that keeps Johnny from reaching his potential.

Many have both spoken and written about the so-called helicopter parent phenomenon. In addition to blaming teachers instead of looking in the mirror or encouraging their children to do so, helicopter parents may go so far as writing students' term papers and fighting battles for them when they need to be assertive. One of my banking clients told me the true story of a new employee's mother who asked if she could "attend her son's first performance appraisal."

Diane Dreher and her associates conducted a study that identifies the characteristics of students with helicopter parents and developed a "controlling parents scale" to measure these factors. They found that students with controlling parents had a high degree of emotional immaturity. Insecure and unable to make decisions for themselves, they had a significantly high external locus of control. The researchers also found that these students were significantly low in optimism and hope, as well as the ability to set goals, make plans, and follow through. Dreher says in a July 27, 2015, *Psychology Today* blog that "these results are disturbing, since research has linked external locus of control with poor mental and physical health and hope is essential to academic success, social success, and overall well-being as well as preventing depression and suicide" (https://www.psychology today.com/us/blog/your-personal-renaissance/201507 /what-helicopter-parents-need-know).

The consequence of having a seismic shift toward victim thinking means more of us feel that the future is not in our hands but in the hands of forces outside ourselves. And since an internal locus of control is positively correlated with happiness, success, and initiative, while an external locus of control is related to anxiety and depression, it's pretty clear that most organizations and society as a whole would be better off if more of us believed we could change things. If we are going to step up, we first have to have a mind shift, from one in which we believe that things are controlled *out there* to the idea that things are in *our* control.

The World Is Neither Innie or Outie

Having said all this, it is important to recognize that the world is neither innie nor or outie. Sometimes our partner is more to blame for what is happening in our relationship, sometimes our competitors do have an unfair advantage, and it's possible that Johnny isn't as much the problem as his teacher. Put aside for a moment whether it is more Johnny or the system that is to blame, and ask this question instead: Which will benefit Johnny more in his adult life; working on his part of the problem or learning from his parents that when things go wrong it is someone else's fault? Ask yourself, What will help you more: focusing on what you can change or on the things outside your control that limit you?

External events do determine some amount of our success and happiness. Your boss may be a jerk and so may be your husband. Some people do get all the breaks. Many factors outside your personal control do drive the great problems of our age. Global warming did not happen just because you took your gas guzzler on a trip that you did not need to take this morning. But the point is that when we focus on what *we* can change, rather than how the rest of the world must change, we feel more in control. Besides—and this really matters—you are the only one you can control anyway!

As my friend Matt pointed out when he had a total jerk for a boss, "I spent months fighting the fact that she had a personality disorder, but everything changed when I started asking myself how I had to adapt to work with a boss like her."

In every situation we may be only 10 percent responsible for what is happening, but when we focus on how we can change our part, our perspective changes. Research has shown that one of the best predictors of successful salespeople, as one example, is that they rarely focus on the external factors influencing their results. Since they cannot control outside forces, they put effort to influence the things they can change.

The good news is that research suggests we can shift from an outward to an inward focus so we can learn to harness the power of responsibility.

Here is a great example of what happens when you choose to be an *innie*. A client of mine, a telecommunications company in the eastern United States, has many of its retail wireless stores in poor retail spaces with leases that cannot be broken. The managers of those stores had every reason to blame the external environment for their poor results compared with the newer stores in better locations. Most of the managers moaned about their bad luck and put in their time waiting to snag an assignment at a better location. But one manager focused on the 10 percent he could influence.

He challenged his people not to act like victims but to ask what they could do in spite of the constraints of a poor location. He engaged his employees in going out to find the customers rather than staying in the stores waiting for customers to arrive. He told his staff, "We can't do anything about our location but we can decide not to be victims." They brainstormed ways to be successful in spite of the location by taking personal initiative. They got involved in the community and met the customers where they were located. They started volunteering as a team at local events and advertising in the process. They even started changing tires for people in parking lots and doing random acts of kindness. They gave out cards in lobbies of local office buildings. In the end, their results beat out most of the stores with much better locations, in large part because they took responsibility for what they could fix rather than focus on the external forces that were out of their control.

Is Your Mindset Fixed or Flexible?

Here is another bit of research to add into the mix. It's not just how we see the world but how we see ourselves that influences whether we step up. Research on the concept of mindset by Carol Dweck, a professor at Stanford University, shows that some of us have a *flexible* mindset while others have a *fixed* mindset, and this mindset may help explain why some of us are more successful. She discovered that those of us with a fixed mindset tend to think of ourselves as having an unchanging set of talents and gifts, and those with a flexible mindset tend to think that we can grow and learn new skills.

In her fascinating research with elementary-age students, Dweck discovered that when children were praised for their effort, regardless of how difficult the task or how well they performed objectively, they would take on harder tasks in order to improve. Those praised for their natural aptitude tended to take on easier tests after being praised. As Po Bronson reported in the February 11, 2007, edition of *New York* magazine, the researchers in one study took one child at a time out of a classroom and gave the child a nonverbal IQ test consisting of a series of puzzles easy enough that all the children would do fairly well. Once the child finished, the researchers gave each student the score and a single line of praise. Randomly divided into groups, some were told, "You must be smart at this." Other students were told, "You must have worked really hard."

Then the students were given a choice of test for the second round. One choice was a more difficult test, but the researchers told the kids that they'd learn a lot from attempting the puzzles. The other choice, Dweck's team explained, was an easy test, just like the first. Of those praised for their effort, 90 percent chose the harder set of puzzles. Of those praised for their intelligence, a majority chose the easy test. The "smart" kids took the easy way out. It was almost as if those praised for being smart did not want to take any risk of blowing that label, and those praised for their effort kept taking on more risk, believing they could stretch.

This research, described in detail in Dweck's book *Mindset: The New Psychology of Success* (Ballantine, 2007), has a great deal of consequence in an organization or a school. If we want people to step up and change things, we need to make sure we praise them for the effort, not just the outcome. When people believe that effort, rather than some set of innate skills or talents, leads to success, they step up and try harder. Guess what happens when we think of ourselves as people who can develop new sets of skills, talents, and aptitudes? We take on the risks involved in doing so. (Read more at Dweck's website, www.mindsetworks.com.)

My daughter, Lena, was an art teacher in the public school system in Chicago. I find her artistic capacity ironic as neither her mother nor I have any seeming aptitude in this area. In fact, since I was very young, I assumed that I had no artistic ability. Given this background, I was fascinated by research Dweck references where students who believe they have little or no artistic talent can be transformed in one week to paint reasonably good paintings. She says the students go from producing paintings in the first class that look like those of first graders to creating paintings that seem quite good to the untrained eye.

As we are with locus of control, most of us are somewhere between the mindset extremes. At times, we get in a fixed mindset, believing that our talents, skills, and aptitudes are frozen at a certain level. To be sure, there are limits to how much we can grow. I love basketball, but I won't ever be Michael Jordan. Still, most of us limit our growth by falling back on the notion that "this is just the way I am."

When we combine a fixed mindset with victim thinking, chances are pretty good that we won't step up. Locus of control is about how we see the world, and mindset is about how we see ourselves. If we believe we can't change, then why step up and try to improve ourselves? If we believe that external events shape the future, why step up and try to initiate change around you?

Changing Your Brain by Stepping Up

It is not entirely clear to me how we change from being victims to being initiators. But I have a strong suspicion that, just as with other activities involving the mind, practice makes perfect. As

Alvaro Pascual Leone of Harvard, one of the world's foremost neuroscientists, told me, "From a brain perspective, every time we do something we are more likely to do it again, and every time we stop ourselves from doing something we are less likely to do it again." In fact, we now know that the human brain evolves and changes during our lifetimes based on our experiences.

Every time we act like a victim or give in to the fixed mindset about ourselves, we reinforce that behavior and thinking, and every time we decide to step up and take responsibility, we increase the chances that we will do so in the future. It is quite possible that by stepping up and taking responsibility we are creating new neuro-connections, literally changing our brains in the process!

Are You Going to Be a Victim or an Actor?

Perhaps we regularly should ask ourselves these questions: Am I going to be a victim or an actor in the various scripts I find myself in today? Will I ask first what I can do to make things better or be content to blame others? Will I accept that I am simply not good at this or choose to believe that hard work and effort will reward me with new skills I did not even know I had? Stepping up is about seeing yourself and others as capable of initiating change. It is about believing that things can be better if we put our minds to it and that reality is mostly of our own making.

But how do we get ourselves or someone we know to make the shift? There are two questions that guide us toward the shift to responsibility. The first one is, What part am I playing? That is the question my friend Matt asked when he finally realized that maybe his boss wasn't the entire problem. The moment we ask what part we are playing or ask that question of someone we are coaching, this is the beginning of going innie.

The second question is, What can I do about it? It is not enough to recognize our part, we must then focus on what actions are in our power to change. A prescription for unhappiness (and suboptimal success) is to focus on things we can't change or things that others need to do. Once again, the same is true when we are coaching othes. By asking them what "they can do," we take them toward their power and away from a passive stance.

This, of course, can change our careers and our lives. Those who say, "It is my job, it was my doing, and let's do what we can to start fixing this" are also the kind of people who tend to get ahead in organizations. Being a person who says "It is my job, let me do what I can, let's get out and change things" gets you promoted and noticed; it's that simple. It may even improve your relationships and help you make a bigger difference *in the world.*

Ways to Step Up

✔ **Banish victim thinking and acting from your life.**
Every time you are tempted to think that something
has been done to you, ask what you can do with what
you have. Outside forces affect our destiny, but we
cannot control these things. Choose to focus on what
you can control.

✔ **Challenge fixed mindset thinking.** Finish this sentence:
I am not ____. You might say you are not romantic, a
people person, a good parent, assertive, and so on.
Then, turn your statement around: *With effort I can be
more romantic, more a people person, more assertive,
and so on.* Choose not to give in to a fixed mindset
about yourself. Do the same with others and your
organization. Instead of saying they will never change,
they will never be different, choose to shift your thinking toward what might change.

✔ **Help your children focus on how they can adapt rather
than blame.** Sure, they will meet people who will
sabotage their success, but focusing on how they can
adapt will help them achieve greater success, whatever
circumstances they find themselves in.

CHAPTER 3

I Am Only One Person or Why People Don't Step Up

*Never doubt that a small group of thoughtful, committed
citizens can change the world. Indeed, it is the only thing
that ever has.*

Margaret Mead, noted anthropologist

It seemed to me that stepping up to initiate change should
be a very natural thing for each of us to do. So as I began to
research and explore the concept of stepping up, I naturally
began to ask myself, why don't we often claim our power to
change things? What keeps us on the sidelines rather than
stepping up to create change?

My publisher, Berrett-Koehler, conducted an online survey to try to understand why we don't step up. We asked a
simple question: why don't you step up? The responses from
325 people across the United States and Canada, most of
whom are professionals, revealed
four primary reasons people say
they don't step up (fig. 1). The
number one answer was "belief I
can't change things/I am only one
person" (46 percent), followed
by the belief that it is "others'
responsibility to change things"
(20 percent), "getting caught up
in the daily grind" (18 percent),

Figure 1.
Why People Don't Step Up

and the "fear of looking bad if I try and nothing changes" (16 percent).

The Power of Aggregate Influence: Why We Think We Can't Change Things

Let's start with the most common response, the belief that things can't change and that "I am only one person." One thing that keeps us from stepping up is the belief that one person cannot really do much. Even those who have stepped up and done great things have often wondered what one person can really do. As one person I interviewed told me, "I know what I have done is just a drop in a bucket, one that has lots of holes in it."

Yet history shows us that one person often makes a huge difference and that behind most great change was one person or a small group of people who got the ball rolling. One reason we may feel disempowered about stepping up is that we forget to factor in what I call *aggregate influence*. We look at our own small actions, and they feel insignificant in the big scheme of things, but we forget that our influence is very large when aggregated with the actions of others. The paradox of such aggregate influence is that while real change is often dependent on many people taking action, in the end this aggregate influence requires each individual to act.

Here are a few simple examples. I live in a neighborhood in the middle of a large city. Partly because many tourists and other visitors (along with many homeless people) walk through our community, there is lots of litter in my neighborhood. To keep the neighborhood clean, I almost always pick up garbage when I walk around.

On the one hand, my actions as one person have little impact on the cleanliness of my community. Yet if even

10 percent of the people in my neighborhood behaved as I do, there is little doubt that such aggregate influence would make for a very tidy place. The paradox is that I can control only my own actions and am only one person, but the aggregate influence of lone individuals like me is significant.

The same is true in an organization. Let's say your company has a poor brand image when it comes to providing personal, caring service. You decide you want to do something about it but think, "I am only one person." Imagine what would happen if even 10 percent of the people in your organization made it their mission to change the image your customers have of your enterprise. Your stepping up may not change things, but when aggregated with the efforts of others, the image of an entire brand can be transformed.

Let's take a larger problem. The oceans of our planet are in increasingly poor condition. The two main contributors to the state of the oceans are overfishing and garbage. Around the world, even in the most remote places such as Midway Island which is over two thousand miles from the nearest continent, birds and sea life choke on garbage that people throw into the oceans. This garbage is mostly made up of plastics that do not biodegrade. The most visible symbol of this issue is called the Great Pacific Garbage Patch, an area where trash has accumulated in the Pacific Ocean more or less the size of Texas. That's right, *Texas*!

The best way to imagine this garbage patch is as a loose but coherent set of floating garbage that has been collecting since the 1950s. The environmental risks posed by the Great Pacific Garbage Patch are significant. The area supports minimal marine life, but birds, sea mammals, and fish mistake the garbage for food (check out www.albatrossthefilm.com). The garbage carries a hidden payload: oily toxins that have accumulated in the plastics. The plastics appear to absorb and concentrate these toxins, which are eaten by unwitting sea creatures. Ultimately, the toxins wind up being recycled inside of us when we eat the seafood.

It is estimated that eight million tons of plastic garbage wind up in the ocean every year and that by 2050 there will be more plastic in the ocean than fish. Some scientists suggest that there are already more parts per million of plastic in the ocean than plankton, the basic food source of the marine system. Millions of marine birds and mammals die every year from ingesting plastic.

What can one person do about all this garbage choking the oceans? Well, if you think about it, this is a problem that can be solved *only* one person at a time. That is why, whenever I am on a beach or even on a street where garbage might fall into a storm drain, I make it my job to pick it up. That is why in 2008, long before many people were thinking about plastic pollution, I took a simple pledge that I hope you will take: no plastic straws, no plastic water bottles, and no plastic shopping bags. I know I am only one person and in one sense my actions are insignificant. But the aggregate influence of one person by the millions being careful about what they throw into the oceans, rivers, and lakes is beyond measure. In fact, no government or the United Nations can solve the problem of garbage in the oceans; it can be solved only by one person times many stepping up.

Two Powerful Examples of Aggregate Influence

Doubt one person can matter? Take the case of Afroz Shah. I first met Afroz in Bangkok, Thailand, where we were both speaking at a sustainability conference. He is a constitutional lawyer in India who moved back to his childhood community of Versova Beach in Mumbai, India, in 2015. Upon his return to the community, he visited the beach upon which he played as a child only to find the shoreline completely covered in garbage, mostly plastic, five feet high! Basically, the beach of his childhood memory had become a carpet of plastic. Afroz and a neighbor began spending Sundays picking up the garbage. He would eventually go door to door and ask others for help.

Word spread and community members began joining his crusade. While he kept at his day job, Afroz has spent over two hundred weekends cleaning up the beach, which by 2018 was finally free of plastic garbage and to which sea turtles returned after years of absence. He would go on to be named a United Nations Champion of the Earth (and later a top ten CNN Hero), and his movement is spreading across India.

Afroz has a Gandhi-like quality about him, and the first time we met was on the evening of my arrival in Bangkok. We hit it off immediately, and he invited me to his room for a long late-night chat about stepping up. "It is ironic," he told me, "that I was named a Champion of the Earth for something we all should do, which is just to step up and fix a problem that is in front of us."

But Afroz's story illustrates the power of one person choosing to act. The moment one person steps up, it creates a powerful ripple that calls others to step up. While Afroz alone cleaning up the beach on weekends would have changed little, the aggregate influence of all of those who joined him made a huge difference.

While we were in Bangkok, Afroz led a small group of us to spend an evening cleaning garbage from a local river. We knocked on the door of a local resident, and Afroz simply did what he had done in India. He told the resident who he was and what he was doing and asked the person to join us. His story, and more importantly, his way of being, is a witness to what must happen whenever people step up.

He also told me "you cannot get people to step up unless you recognize that they have the right not to step up. I never tell someone what they must do. Instead I take action and then invite them to join me."

Another great example is Beth Terry, a California accountant who read an article in 2007 about the garbage patch and saw pictures of birds in the south Pacific choking on plastic bottle tops and toothbrushes. She was only one person but set herself on a campaign to rid her life of as much plastic as possible and began blogging about her personal efforts (www .myplasticfreelife.com). Though she still makes her living as an accountant, she has become a regular media spokesperson, has been featured by the likes of *Ladies Home Journal* and ABC News, and personally spearheaded a campaign to get Clorox to create a recycling program for its Brita water filters, which until then could not be recycled. She was only one person but that hasn't stopped her from making a huge difference. By the way, forty million water bottles are thrown out every day in the world or over ten billion a year!

What If We Step Up and Nothing Changes?

About one-sixth of the people who answered our survey said that fear of failure was another reason they won't or don't step up. What if we step up and nothing changes? After all, for every person who stepped up and changed things, there must be many others who tried and fell short. What if I change myself, and my partner does not make changes? What if I step up and try to take initiative in my company, and others don't? What if I try to change something about myself, but find that, in spite of my best efforts, I don't get better?

It is true that if we step up there is no guarantee that things will change. You may step up and change yourself, but your marriage may fail anyway; you may try to rally your colleagues to improve morale without achieving the end result; and you might give up water bottles and pick up garbage to keep it from going into the sea, but that garbage whirlpool might grow anyway.

But here is the truth: **there is a 100 percent guarantee that nothing will change if you don't step up.** What's more, we are much more likely to regret having stayed on the sidelines than we are to regret our failures. This is something I learned when I interviewed older people for my bestselling book *The Five Secrets You Must Discover Before You Die;* people rarely regret their failures but often regret not trying.

A woman recently talked to me about her failed marriage and how hard she had tried toward the end to change herself. Even though she felt her husband was more to blame, she decided to work hard on changing her own patterns of behaving and relating. She told me, "When it ended, I did not have any regrets because I knew I had done everything I could have done to change myself to make things better."

Ken Lyotier is a man you will read about in more detail later in this book. His odds of succeeding would have been pegged somewhere near zero. He told me, "At some point in our lives we have to take the risk of believing we can change things. Even if you don't succeed, you might inspire others to try. There is a force in all of us that wants to just sit on the sofa, get a beer, and watch the football game instead of believing and risking. The risk we are afraid of is that we will step up and won't find anything, but if you just sit, there is a guarantee that you won't."

This is the challenge each of us faces—to take the risk to step up even though we know we may fail, or to sit on the sofa and talk about how things might have been different had we stepped up.

Holding back has its rewards. When we hold back, we can always protect our ego, telling ourselves that if we had really tried, who knows what might have happened? It is not hard to understand why we hold back since none of us enjoys failing. But failure is not the worst thing that can happen to a person. In fact, some of those who stepped up and made the biggest difference often experienced multiple failures along the way.

But I Am Too Busy to Step Up!

Another reason people (18 percent) told me they don't step up is that they are simply too caught up in the daily grind. We are often simply too busy getting through the tasks of our daily life or work to step out of that routine to try to influence change. Can it really be that we are simply too busy to step up and make a difference?

Busyness is often the greatest barrier to legacy in its many forms. It is easy to let trivial matters fill our calendars and days rather than focusing on making a difference. Even as I write this chapter, my email inbox is filled with scores of messages relating to trivial matters. But three emails relate to a nonprofit board on which I serve, an organization that serves homeless people in my community. The organization is in desperate need of reimagining its vision and has asked me to help. That work will not pay the bills nor is it clawing at me with any urgency compared with the trivial emails, but I am pretty certain that stepping up to help that board could actually lead to things being different in some small way in the city where I live. This is the choice we must often make, between legacy and the immediate, between what claws at us and what calls to us.

What have you been meaning to step up to do that keeps getting sidelined by the deceptively urgent and ultimately trivial?

My friend Jeremy has a full life of family obligations and the responsibility of running two businesses. But when his son Robin developed type 1 diabetes as a teenager, he and Robin became aware that the medical help they took for granted was often not available to families in much of the developing world. At Robin's prodding, together they stepped up to initiate an effort to get cities in the developed world to adopt villages in the developing world to provide the skill and resources needed to manage diabetes in their communities. Robin was an active teenager and avid soccer player who was suddenly thrown into a world of needles and restricted diets, but he resisted any temptation to self-pity in favor of helping others, and his father fought the temptation of the daily grind that constantly clawed at him. As I write this they are well on their way to their first type 1 village in Guyana.

Not stepping up because of the tyranny of the daily grind may be the greatest risk of all. It may mean you come to the end of your life or career wondering what might have happened if you had stepped up. You may wind up feeling deeply the words of the late Rabindranath Tagore, Nobel Prize–winning poet in India: "The song that I came to sing remains unsung to this day. I have spent my days in stringing and in unstringing my instrument."

Let Someone Else Do It

Finally, about 20 percent of those who responded said that they don't step up because they believe it is someone else's responsibility to change things. Now, this is one reason that few of us would admit to, but we all know we have given in to this belief.

I realized how easy it is to fall into this trap after having an argument with my wife. I was focused on what my wife needed to do to fix our marriage instead of taking responsibility for my part. The more I focused on what she should do, the less powerful I felt and the less impact I could have. Even if the problem was only 10 percent mine (and I assure you it was far larger than that), by focusing on what I can do instead of what someone else should do is always the right place to begin.

Whenever we focus on what others need to do, we give away our power and let ourselves off the hook. My mother was Canadian and my father American, so I am privileged to be a citizen of both Canada and the United States. Several years ago, I tried without success to lead an effort to get Canadians to take a national pledge of sustainability. The idea was simple: get millions of Canadians to take a pledge to commit to sustainability in our lifetime. Although some people got excited by the prospect, many said, "Canada is so small, what difference would it make if we take this pledge? Look at India and China. That is where you need to focus, because if they don't act we are all doomed."

But I saw the problem differently. It is true that Canada is a relatively small nation with only thirty-three million people, but Canada also has the highest per capita energy use of any country in the world. Besides, those of us living in Canada cannot fix China or India; all we can do is to choose to act right here where we are, trusting others to act in their sphere of influence. We can't fix China or India any more than I could fix my wife or you can change anyone in your company besides yourself.

This gets at the heart of the challenge. It does not matter what anyone else is or is not doing; the place to begin is always right here and right now. This tendency to think that others, instead of us, need to change is both insidious and disempowering.

Howard Behar is the former president of Starbucks International and author with Janet Goldstein of the book *It's Not about the Coffee*. When I interviewed Behar for this book, he told me a story about the first managerial position he had following university, running a furniture store that was part of a family-owned chain. During his first month, the owner of the company, a man well into his seventies, came to visit Behar's store. On his way in from the parking lot, the owner saw a piece of garbage in front of the store and picked it up. Soon, he picked up a tiny cigarette wrapper and then began scraping some chewing gum from the sidewalk outside the store. At that point, Behar said, "Hey, you don't need to do that. I will have someone come pick this up later." The old business owner stood up, looked Behar square in the eye, and said, "Behar, if not me, who? If not now, when?"

Behar said this set him on a lifelong journey of picking up garbage and of refusing to hire employees at Starbucks who didn't see it as their responsibility to pick things up.

What I set out to do is to find people who stepped up and to determine what they had in common. I wanted to understand why some people step up and change things. More importantly, I wanted to understand the secrets to how we can step up. The chapters that follow reveal what I discovered, the secrets to stepping up, and how to make a bigger difference in your sphere of influence.

Ways to Step Up

✔ **Assume that aggregate influence is already happening.**
Whenever you are tempted to think, "I am only one
person," change your thinking to assume that the
aggregate influence is already in process and that
others are already acting or will act. Imagine the
impact of many others stepping up with you.

✔ **Question your hesitation.** When tempted to stay on
the sidelines, ask which you will regret more, trying
without success or holding back. In most cases, thinking
it through causes us to realize that failure or moderate
success is much more palatable than having never tried.

✔ **Focus on the important matters.** As you begin each
day, ask what important matters are being put aside
for trivial matters that seem urgent but are not your
legacy. Focus on your important contribution first, not
around the edges of trivial matters.

CHAPTER 4

Only Naïve People Change the World

*Not much happens without a dream. A dream is
never enough, but for something good to happen
the dream must be there first.*

Robert Greenleaf

Rex Weyler is in his sixties now, but he is showing me a picture of himself in his twenties. In the black-and-white photograph, he looks an awful lot like many of the people I went to university with during the 1970s—he has long, jet black hair tied in a ponytail as he sits with a camera in a rubber Zodiac boat with a large fishing vessel dead ahead.

He is taking me back to a time almost forty years ago when he knows for sure that his stepping up, along with others, helped change the course of history. His story reads like a modern David and Goliath tale and helps illustrate an important principle: if you want to step up and change things, first you have to believe you can. Again and again, as I interviewed people for this book, I was struck by the fact that almost everyone who stepped up and changed things had an unrelenting belief in the possibility of change, even when the odds seemed against it. Even if others told them things would never change, they chose a different path.

To put Rex's story in perspective, we have to go back to the late 1960s and early 1970s. At that time, there was a growing protest movement all over the world, withthe prime areas of focus being peace and civil rights. The women's movement was in full force, and growing numbers of people were standing up and getting their voices heard, often for the first time. The environmental movement on the other hand was in its infancy, with most people focused on the legitimate concerns of people rather than the plight of the planet. Rex muses, "At the time progressive people were mostly focused on people issues, but some people were just starting to see that the ultimate social justice issue was the earth itself. What would it matter if we achieved social justice but ruined the planet?"

One of the most visible environmental issues at the time was the hunting of whales. By the early 1970s, whales had been hunted to the point where only about 5–10 percent of their historic populations remained. Many whale species were on the brink of extinction, and the Atlantic Gray Whale was already gone. A Canadian named Farley Mowat had helped catalyze the issue when he wrote a book titled *A Whale for the Killing*. It told the story of a whale caught in a cove in Newfoundland and how people came down and shot at the whale from the shore. "It was the reverse of the *Moby Dick* story," Rex said. "It is the helpless whale being swallowed up by the people."

Whales were pretty much being hunted for products that could be created synthetically. In other words, the whale hunt was unnecessary. At the same time, a growing body of research showed that whales were actually incredibly intelligent mammals, rather than dumb, uncaring monsters like the whales found in Herman Melville's *Moby Dick*. Much later, we would discover that not only is their brain-to-body-mass larger than that of humans, but that the most-developed part of their brain is the limbic, or emotional, part. Humans were systematically hunting down intelligent, sensitive fellow mammals for no real benefit. Something had to be done.

Rex Weyler and a somewhat disorganized band of hippies and journalists hatched an idea, an idea he admits was a bit crazy. The idea was to go out and confront a whaling ship in the middle of the Pacific Ocean and show the world what was happening. Being journalists, they believed that if you could change the story you could change the world. There were others trying to save the whales but getting no real traction.

In the days before global positioning systems and before CNN, finding whalers was no easy task. After months of frustration on the open ocean, they spotted part of the Russian whaling fleet on the high seas. The idea was simple—catch the whalers in the act. Capture the whale hunt on camera for what it really was. Rex snapped a picture of a beautiful but bloodied whale being harpooned and dragged onto the deck of the vessel. The pictures he and the others took and the story of these not-so-mighty few confronting the Russian whaling fleet appeared in most of the newspapers and magazines across the free world. The story was featured on the evening news across America, including coverage by the well-respected Walter Cronkite at CBS. The story created what Rex calls a *mind bomb* around the world.

"It didn't hurt that we caught the Russians just a few hundred miles off the coast of California during the cold war," he told me. "But what people responded to most was the idea of people stepping up for what they believed in. Today, the idea of average citizens standing up for larger forces has become commonplace, but at the time standing up for another species in such a bold way was virtually unheard of."

The mind bomb did not stop whaling in its tracks, but it raised public awareness about the whale hunt to a new level. Over the next year, others worldwide began to demand that the hunt end. Rex said, "A number of things happen when you take a stand. First it clarifies your own morality, because if you are going to take a stand it forces you to make the case. Second, when you step up, it inspires others, because people are typically better at following than leading. Now people have permission to do so. Immediately, people begin to stand up because they know they won't be alone."

It took several years before the international whaling ban was finally signed and the mass hunting of whales stopped, but if you want to know what began the worldwide movement in earnest—the initial step up that galvanized public opinion about the whales—it can be found in that picture hanging on Rex Weyler's office wall, a black-and-white symbol of what happens when you think you can change things.

Today, Rex's face has aged, but his youthful idealism still radiates when he talks about the issues of the day. He was a pioneer at the organization called Greenpeace, which had a huge impact on saving the whales. You may love the Greenpeace tactics or find them offensive, but if you want to hear all about it, read Rex's 2004 book, *Greenpeace: How a Group of Ecologists, Journalists and Visionaries Changed the World* (Raincoast Books). Whales are still hunted on a limited basis in the guise of research, but populations have rebounded. People are still stepping up to make sure whales continue to thrive. Their populations are threatened now by climate change and toxicity in the ocean environment. As Rex reminded me in our interview, "The bad guys only have to win once."

Reflecting back almost four decades after the mind bomb, I asked the now gray-haired Rex Weyler how it felt to be in his sixties but to know that, at one point in his life, he helped change the course of history.

"Well," he mused, "mostly I think of how crazy we were. I mean, they could just as easily have harpooned us! This is before CNN and twenty-four hour news; we had no news crews tagging alongside. We were really quite naïve."

The moment he said that, I had my own mind bomb: maybe only naïve people ever change the world.

Everything Begins with a Vision

The first step to stepping up is to be naïve enough to think you can change things. This may seem so obvious as not to merit mention, but having a belief that it matters if we step up is critical. Robert Greenleaf, who popularized a leadership philosophy called Servant Leadership, once said, "Not much happens without a dream. A dream is never enough, but for something good to happen the dream must be there first." The leaders I interviewed for this book echoed those sentiments.

As I asked them about people who stepped up and created change, they often talked about people having a vision of how things could be better and believing they could achieve that vision. Don Knauss is the former CEO and executive chairman of Clorox and a former officer in the US Marines who radiates enthusiasm. He told me that "stepping up begins with the belief that you can change things." As he reflected on his own experiences of those who stepped up, he talked about one key being a prevailing optimism, that is, a pervasive belief that if you stay with it you will prevail.

This prevailing optimism drives people to step up most every day on much lower-profile issues than stopping the whale hunt. Bob Peter is the former president of the LCBO, a liquor retailer in Canada and the former president of the Bay, Canada's leading department store. In his many years of leadership he said that again and again he has noticed that the people who step up and make things better have "a vision of how things could be better and an almost little-dog-on-a-bone quality about pursuing that vision." He told me about Nancy Cardinal, who inherited the marketing department at the Liquor Board of Ontario with just three people in it and a brand that was basically just a "building with booze in it."

But Nancy had a vision that a government-run liquor store chain could be a world-class retailer. She helped craft a vision to reimagine the stores, started a food and wine magazine, created signature vintage stores in certain neighborhoods, pushed for wider aisles and better stores, and spearheaded an effort to double the number of female customers. Mostly, she had that same naïve vision of the future that Rex Weyler had of a world with no whale hunting. Where some saw just a government liquor store, she and others at the organization saw a leading retailer on par with the best liquor stores anywhere. Today many of the LCBO stores look more like high-end retail shops than a government liquor store. Much of the credit for the transformation belongs to Nancy, but many others who did not accept the prevailing belief that being a government agency meant being a second-rate retail operation also contributed.

If you want to step up and change things, you first have to believe you can. You have to imagine a positive future and believe that you are someone who can do something about creating that future.

Transforming Inner City Schools in the United States

Earlier, I talked about Mike Feinberg and Dave Levin, who joined the Teach for America program and were placed at two inner city schools in Houston, Texas, starting in August 1992. It was pretty naïve of them to believe that they could personally turn the tide for the low-income kids they were teaching, let alone become a major force for education reform in America. Yet this is just the kind of naïve optimism that shows itself again and again in those who step up.

Not that stepping up is easy. When we read the stories of people who stepped up, it sounds so easy in retrospect, but in real time it often means having a dogged perseverance along with a resolve to turn *no* into *yes*. Mike and Dave had to fight to make their vision a reality. After getting permission to pilot their KIPP classes in Houston, the first two years of the program were a great success, but then Houston had a major space problem. The district superintendent called and said that there was no space for the program to grow. That meant that either KIPP could not take in any new fifth graders, or the seventh graders would have to go back to the normal program. Mike protested, and his boss told him he was being stubborn. In the end she told him that "only the superintendent can fix this."

"The next day," Mike told me, "I went down to the superintendent's office and said I'd like a meeting with Dr. Paige. They basically said go away." Here's what he said happened next: "When I left his office, I figured there has got to be a way to get a meeting. I found his car in the parking lot in the superintendent's spot and sat on the car in the hot sun for four hours grading papers. I figured sooner or later he had to come out of his office. When he saw me he told me to get off the car. I told him why I was there and he told me, 'Look, I believe in what you are doing so come see me tomorrow morning.'

"The next morning I showed up, and my boss and her boss were there. They looked like they wanted to kill me. I pleaded my case. The superintendent said, 'I love this program so, let's

solve this. I have to go negotiate a food contract; you guys figure out how to solve it.' When he left, my boss told me I was
basically a jackass. I said yes I may be, but Dr. Paige said we
need to work it out."

Work it out they did, and the program not only grew but
also has influenced much of the conversation about educational reform in America.

All of us get ideas about how things could be better, but
often we hear another voice that gets in the way. Mike Feinberg
talked to me about a kind of prison that keeps us from stepping up.

"There is a line in *The Matrix* [a 1999 science fiction
movie] about creating a prison for our own mind," he said.
"We all have a voice inside of us that says we can't step up. It
tells us we are not good enough, that we are going to screw
this up, a voice that says how foolish we will look if we fail.
There is another voice alongside it that says you can do it and
that you want to do it. We have to be aware of the voice in our
head that is keeping us prisoner. Make sure you are not selling yourself short. We can accomplish so much more than we
think we can if we are willing to work hard and be as creative
as we can be."

Listening to Mike made me think of something a farmer
friend of mine had told me about cattle. Ranchers used to have
big problems with cows crossing roads until some inventive
person discovered the cattle guard, a small ditch with metal
roller bars that cows will not cross because they feel unstable.
What is really interesting is that an even more inventive person discovered that you don't even have to put in the ditch or
rollers; all you have to do is paint them on the road, and the
cows still won't cross them. Many of us don't step up to change
things because there are paintings of barriers that don't actually exist. In fact, we painted them ourselves!

Naïve Belief in Daily Life

This naïve belief in the possibility of things getting better is as important in daily life as it is in the larger landscapes of stepping up at work and in the world. When we are naïve enough to believe that things can be better, or even that we can be better, things change. We all have an image of ourselves; this is the person we think we are. Sometimes it is a positive image, but other times we limit ourselves with that image.

We say, "I am not an artist, I am not musical, I am not good at relationships, I am not a people person, and I simply don't have the skill that others have." Within organizations we often say things like, "Nothing will ever change around here, I can't make this place better, and things have always been this way." What these people who stepped up show us is that believing we can change and reality can change are prerequisites to stepping up. It is not until we believe a situation can be different that we will step up and try.

Some time ago, I was asked to coach a senior leader in a large company. He was a strategic master, as smart as a whip, and ran a tight ship. The problem was that he, by his own description, was simply not a people person. He had a hard time connecting personally with people, and in meetings he often made others feel deflated by the matter-of-fact way he dissected their work, finding every tiny fault. When he engaged me as a coach, the first thing he said was, "I've never been a good people person. I'm naturally critical and very task oriented. I don't need people to blow sunshine at me, so I don't see the need to blow it at others. Ever since I have been a manager, people have said they admire my smarts but I'm just not warm and fuzzy."

The first thing I told him was that it was going to take a lot of hard work to change those behaviors because he had been doing them for a long time. But I said, "We have to begin with this image you have of yourself. The truth is you don't think you can change, and you have already given yourself every excuse to fail. All your life you've probably been told this is just the way you are. But it is not true. It is just the way you are right now."

I asked him to write up a vision of himself in the future, what he would be like in six months.

To be honest, everyone in the organization pegged the odds of success at near zero. One of his colleagues told me, "Bill is just a smart jerk. It's that simple." Six months later, that same colleague told me, "I can't believe this is the same guy." It took a lot of hard work, that little-dog-on-a-bone quality that Bob Peter talked to me about. But I honestly believe the big leap was Bill's willingness to be a little naïve about the possibility of change. He had to decide that he could be different.

No one thought a group of volunteers could stop the whale hunt or that two teachers could turn inner city students and schools into top performers. No one thought a government liquor store could become a top-notch retailer. No one thought Versova Beach in Mumbai would ever be free of plastic garbage. But Rex Weyler believed the whale hunt could be stopped, Mike Feinberg believed that inner city schools could succeed, Nancy Cardinal saw a great retailer where others saw a government liquor store, and Afroz Shah believed he could galvanize an entire community to care about cleaning up the oceans.

What image of yourself do you need to throw out so you can step up and change yourself? What situation at work or in your life do you believe can't be fixed (and is that belief keeping you on the sidelines)?

Ways to Step Up

✔ **Remind yourself that only naïve people ever change things.** Remind yourself every time you think something can't be different, whether it is yourself or a situation. Decide to take a step instead of focusing on what can't be done.

✔ **Challenge assumptions.** Every time someone says, "Things will never change," make it your mission to challenge that assumption.

✔ **Disregard the voice.** Every time you hear a voice inside yourself saying, "It won't matter if I step up," take the step anyway.

CHAPTER 5

The 100/0 Principle:
100 Percent Responsibility/
Zero Excuses

*There are always constraints. The question
is what will you do in spite of them.*

In 1998, a relatively unknown bank, Synovus, was named the best company to work for in America by *Fortune* magazine. Each year, *Fortune* compiles a list of the one hundred best companies to work for, and to be named the very best among thousands of contenders is quite an honor. Given that I had never heard of the bank, I decided to do some research on this "best company to work for in America." What I discovered was a hundred-year-old bank that had grown like a wildfire throughout the southern United States, a company that had an enviable record of double-digit profit growth and that was beating the pants off much bigger banks in most of their markets. Needless to say, I was intrigued.

Three months later, I was sitting in the office of then-CEO Jimmy Blanchard, who had been CEO for over thirty years at the time. When I asked him the bank's secret and why it might have been named the best company to work for in America, he offered a simple reason: "It is the power of love. We are successful because we love each other, and we love our customers.

When one part of this company cries, the whole company cries with them. We love our customers and each other; it's that simple." Then he set me loose to talk to others throughout the bank and its subsidiaries.

Over the next few days I heard an awful lot about love, but I also kept hearing people talk about a concept called *100/0*. Finally, I asked a teller in one of the branches, "What is the 100/0?" She said, "The 100 stands for 100 percent responsibility. You never say, 'This would be a great bank if the CEO did his job,' 'I'd have made the deadline if not for the other department,' 'I would be having a better day if my boss was nicer,' or 'It's not my job to take care of that customer.'" She said all employees had to take 100 percent responsibility for themselves and for the success of this bank because, "It is up to each one of us to keep this company great and keep the customers happy. And the zero," she said, "that stands for no excuses. There are always reasons you did not come through, but at the end of the day you work with what you have, so there are no excuses for not giving your best."

In a meeting a day later I asked Jimmy Blanchard that if the secret to the bank was the "power of love," then what was with the 100/0? He replied, "Well, I guess it is tough love."

After leaving the bank it occurred to me that those two numbers are transformative. For a company, for a person, and maybe for the world! When we take 100 percent responsibility and give ourselves no excuses for why we can't or shouldn't act to make things different, everything changes.

I can't tell you how many times I have seen people turn those numbers around. There are lots of 0/100 people in the world. It seems as though they don't think anything is their responsibility, and they have all kinds of excuses why they can't change. People say things like these: my marriage would sure be better if she would be different; morale around here stinks, and I sure wish the manager would do something about it, but I'm not going to take any action until he does; my restaurant is not doing very well, but we are in a bad location, and the place is kind of run down; if the company would just spend some money, business would pick up. Bottom line: it is not my fault, and here is the long list of reasons why I can't do anything about it.

There is a disease of 0/100 thinking in our society. No excuses may seem a bit extreme, but the point is not so much that there are never any constraints but that there are *always* constraints that could keep us from stepping up. When we focus on those constraints instead of on what we can do given those constraints, we wind up acting like victims. Make no mistake, your career will be very limited if you become known as one of those people who always has a reason why they did not come through.

When I interviewed CEOs and senior executives for this book, they told me that people who always have a reason for not coming through drive them crazy. Don Knauss, the CEO of Clorox, summed up the feelings of many of those executives I interviewed: "What really drives me nuts is when people rationalize losing. There is a real sickness in organizations around rationalizing losing."

Don't get me wrong. I am not saying that constraints aren't real or that there is never a legitimate reason for failure. I am saying that if we decide to work with whatever deck we have been dealt and go from there, we will accomplish much more. Another way I like to think of it is this: Some excuses are true, but none of them are useful. Focusing on what you can change is useful, but focusing on the reasons you can't succeed or act is wasted energy.

A Woman Who Had Every Excuse to Fail...
but Didn't

Here is a case in point. Joanne Beaton wanted to get back into operations inside her company but did not anticipate the assignment she received. She was asked to take over the operator services business for TELUS, a large telecommunications company in Canada. It was hardly a plum assignment. For one thing, it was a dying part of the industry, since just about everyone could see that technology eventually would replace human beings for most of the functions operators once played in the telephone business. Long gone were the days when every call went through a human interface or even when calling Information was the main route to find phone numbers. The service was losing money and losing steam. In fact, most TELUS competitors in telecommunications were trying to outsource operator services to reduce the cost of providing those services.

The attractiveness of the assignment was hardly enhanced by the workforce she inherited. Engagement and morale were low. She was told that the one thousand or so workers, mostly unionized, were deeply in an entitlement mentality and waiting for someone else to fix their eroding business. Her leaders told her that the most likely ultimate solution was to outsource the business, but in the meantime her marching orders were to cut costs. Some colleagues wondered aloud why she would take such a tough assignment.

Joanne had every good excuse to follow the natural path of reducing costs and eventually getting some outside vendor to do it cheaper. There was every reason to think the business would die a slow death. That is probably what would have happened in most cases. But that is not what happened. It is not even in the ballpark of what happened.

The no excuses part of 100/0 means that we begin by not surrendering to the excuses that could keep us from stepping up. No excuses means recognizing that while some excuses may be true, they are almost never useful. The question is always, What are you going to do *in spite* of those constraints?

Joanne says the difference between a good leader and a *really* good leader is that the really good leaders ask, "What can I do with the constraints?" while others come up with reasons why they could not, did not, deliver what they said they could.

Joanne Beaton and her team worked with the constraints. Some people might not have seen it as their responsibility to save that declining business for TELUS, but she did. When Joanne took over as leader, some people on the team had an alternative idea of the future, however unlikely it seemed. They believed that they could become the place where others brought their outsourced operator services. Even though the company had dabbled in those waters, the idea seemed far-fetched, given the cost structure and employees' low level of engagement.

Joanne met with every team member at operator services and basically said, "No one else is going to save this business but us." She encouraged employees to act like owners and asked them to consider this question: if you were the competition, what would you do to put us out of business? She pretty much said, "Let's go big or go home." She said they had a choice to be outsourced or to step up and make theirs the best operator services in the world, so good that it would be the *outsourcer* instead of the *outsourced*. And she emphasized, "If we want to become the outsourcer instead of the outsourced, we will have to take responsibility and make it happen. No one else will do it. We need to save ourselves!"

Well, the team did take responsibility and threw out the excuses. The team, not the leader, came up with a simple theme: Our Business, Our Customers, Our Team, and My Responsibility. To save their business all employees had to step up and ask what they could do to make the business successful. They realized that they needed to make it happen. And they did.

They began to benchmark their services against competitors, talked about how to improve the business, and figured out how to raise morale and productivity. Within three years, the engagement scores of this work unit went from low to supercharged! Not only did their jobs not get outsourced, but they grew the business threefold, increased their productivity by 1,000 percent, and became a high-service, low-cost operator. Eventually, they won awards for the best operator services in North America and became a sustainable profit center! TELUS operator services became a major provider of operator services for many of their competitors. Headcount grew fourfold instead of shrinking. They transformed a dying business into a growing enterprise.

As Joanne looks back on this experience, she says, "People had told me we have been trying for eight years to shift this, these folks can't change. But I did not accept the story." And when people on her team pointed fingers at others, she kept putting it back on them. "I kept telling them, look stop blaming others, let's take the levers we can move and do it." Joanne makes it clear, "I was the leader, but everyone stepped up and took responsibility, and that is why we succeeded."

Years later, in 2005, a customer call center within the same company was in a similarly tough position. Rumors said the company was considering closing down the call center in a remote community, which made sense as it was the last call center outside a major urban area. The leaders and employees in that business unit could have acted 0/100, coming up with lots of reasons to sit back and accept their likely fate. But that is not what happened.

A few key frontline supervisors stepped up and asked for a meeting with senior managers in the company. They said, "What do we need to do so you won't close us down?" As is often the case, a few people began what later became a ripple. Notice that people who step up focus not on what someone else will do for them, but on what they can do for themselves. The senior leaders, impressed with the supervisors' initiative but unsure of the ultimate outcome, said, "If you create a highly productive and engaged call center focused on great service, we'd be fools to close you down." And that is exactly what they did.

Groups of employees began to meet with managers to ask everyone to step up. They worked hard to create an infectious spirit and eventually became one of the most highly engaged work units in the company with over 90 percent of their team members giving high scores on the companywide employee engagement survey. Considering that call centers provide notoriously low-morale, high-turnover jobs, this was no small feat. The spirit became so infectious that the company kept its word. Not only did company leaders not close the call center, but they also recently made a series of significant investments to grow that center as a reward for those employees and managers' stepping up. Bottom line: we can either sit around and be victims or ask what we can do to change things. Which do you think the world rewards?

How 100/0 Changes Everything

If you doubt the power of these two numbers, 100/0, for even a moment, think about this. How would your company be different if all employees felt 100 percent responsible for the company morale, for the image of the brand, for cutting costs, for their own happiness and careers, and for winning customers? What if instead of looking for someone else to solve a problem, they just began by asking themselves what they can do personally to make things better?

When the employee survey numbers came back, imagine if all team members asked both how they had contributed to the current level of engagement and how they could make things better. Of course, senior managers in a company have a big influence, and there are real constraints that get in the way of stepping up. But when all employees step up and take responsibility for what they can do, the energy shifts.

How might your company—or even your life—be different if you decided not to surrender to your excuses? What would happen if we realized that there are always constraints, and the only question was, How will we work to accomplish our goals given those constraints? Joanne Beaton's team could not change the fact that operator services was and is a dying business, but by not giving in to that story they focused on stepping up in spite of it.

Think about the impact of those two numbers in a marriage (or in any relationship in our personal or work lives). As was mentioned earlier, in my first career as a Presbyterian minister, I was often called upon to counsel couples who were having trouble in their relationships. Never once in those seven years did a couple arrive with one partner saying, "Wait. Before we even start, I want you to know it's me who needs to change." The pervasive norm was the polar opposite, with each person arriving with fingers wagging at the other—*if she would just*... and *if he would just*... then everything would be better.

Now I will grant you as an objective outsider that it often seemed to me as if one person was a little, and sometimes a lot, more responsible. But what I discovered was that if I could get people to look at themselves instead of at the other person, the whole energy shifted. If they said there was not a lot of romance, I would ask, "So tell me what you think you can to bring more romance into the relationship?" It really does not matter what percentage of any problem is created by you; all that really matters is whether you are doing what you can to make it better. One hundred percent responsibility; it's that simple.

It may be a natural human tendency to focus on what *they* need to do, but trust me, you will be a lot happier if you focus on what *you* can do. When you find yourself focusing on an excuse as to why you can't succeed—whatever excuse it might be—ask if the excuse is useful instead of asking if it is true. What would you do in spite of that excuse to get what you want?

Let me give you a personal example. Historically, I have not been a good networker, which is not a good thing when you run your own business. Once I have a relationship with someone I am very social, but I have a strong fear of reaching out to people I don't know well. I have a whole list of excuses, all of which are true, for why I am not a good networker: I am shy by nature, did not have good mentors, I had bad acne in high school that played havoc with my self-esteem. All of these excuses are true, valid, and help explain my poor track record as a networker. They also all happen to be useless. The more I focus on them, the more I let myself off the hook. Excuses may be true, but they are rarely useful. Focusing on our excuses, even when they are legitimate, merely locks us into a cycle of inaction.

Part of being 100/0 is a willingness to look in the mirror first, instead of looking outside. When we look inside, we move to a place of responsibility instead of blame. When we take responsibility, full responsibility, for every problem, even if we are only a small contributor, everything changes.

Let's look at two real life examples of what happens when we take responsibility and when we don't. A friend of mine is the CEO of a nonprofit. It is his first assignment in such a senior position, and about a year after he became the CEO he ran into some trouble. His board called him to task and basically told him that he needed to make some pretty significant changes in his behavior or they would let him go. At first, his reaction was defensive, 0/100 if you will. He focused on the organization, on its challenging history, and on a few key board members who were dysfunctional. Soon, however, he came to an important realization.

First, he could not fix them any more than you can fix your wife, your husband, your boss, the economy, your history. Second, if he chose a path of self-reflection, this situation could provide a meaningful learning opportunity for him. Instead of focusing on what they were doing, he focused on his part of the problem. He sought feedback, listened without becoming defensive, and asked for board members' help. He took 100 percent responsibility for the situation. Right now, he and the board are back on track, and most everyone who works with him says he is a better leader than he was before.

The second example has a far less happy ending. Another friend was executive director at a different nonprofit. He felt he was being questioned by his board and blew up several times during meetings, showing some significant emotional immaturity. He bristled when the board wanted to give him some difficult feedback. This executive stayed focused on what others had done to him. Admittedly, he had a somewhat dysfunctional board, but it was no more dysfunctional than many boards. Also, the board had not provided good guidance or feedback for him. But because he never owned his part and stayed focused on what others were doing—rather than on what he could do—the situation deteriorated. Eventually he had to resign.

I am convinced that both of these executives were equally competent, their situations equally redeemable. One chose 100/0, and one chose 0/100. One is gainfully employed now and the other is not.

True Grit

This capacity to work through challenges is probably one of the most underestimated competencies of successful people, which is why I am fascinated by the work of Angela Duckworth, author of *Grit: The Power of Passion and Perseverance*. She has studied a concept she calls *grit*, which she defines as "the tendency to pursue long-term challenging goals with perseverance and passion." Much of grit as Duckworth has defined it involves the willingness to work hard through adversity to achieve success. She has published a series of journal articles studying this concept and produced a series of videos that you can find on YouTube. One fine article is "Deliberate Practice Spells Success: Why Grittier Competitors Triumph at the National Spelling Bee," published in 2010 in *Social Psychological and Personality Science*.

Her research has shown that grit is a better predictor than intelligence of grade point average, retention at the US Military Academy in West Point, and ranking in the national spelling bee. That is, the capacity to work through adversity is a pretty good predictor of success in most any endeavor. Getting started is one thing but staying with a goal even when it gets hard may be the real trick to stepping up.

Rex Weyler and his compatriots did not find the Russian whaling fleet with ease. They endured months of planning, hard disappointments, and moments at sea feeling literally and figuratively lost. If it sounds as though Joanne Beaton and her team at TELUS cruised in turning that business around, think again. There were moments of despair and many times when it looked as if things might not work out. Stepping up requires grit, a willingness to work through the hard times and stay focused on your goal.

To step up and change things we need first to have vision and a naïve belief that things can change, but we also need to take 100 percent responsibility. There will be constraints. Things will get in the way. You will have excuses, but none of them will help you. So repeat after me: "I can change things, and I will take responsibility."

I am fond of quoting John Wooden on this matter. Wooden happens to have won more national championships than any coach in US men's college basketball history. He once said, "Things turn out best for those who make the most of how things turn out."

Ways to Step Up

✔ **Determine your part.** Whenever you encounter a problem, ask yourself what you have done to contribute to the problem. Then ask, "What can I do to change the situation?"

✔ **Don't make excuses.** Next time you are given a tough assignment, don't make excuses as to why you can't succeed. The odds are pretty good that your boss or others already know about the constraints and will be more impressed with your willingness to try than with your list of reasons for failure.

✔ **Work through adversity.** Most everyone who steps up and accomplishes anything had to endure setbacks along the way. Grit may be one of the most important characteristics of people who step up and make things happen. Next time you experience a setback on your way to achieving something, ask yourself, "How else can I get this done?" There is a time to raise the white flag of surrender, but most of us raise it far too soon.

CHAPTER 6

Do Something—
Do Anything

*If you wait for the perfect plan, you may be
waiting forever.*

A few years ago, a foundation in the United States ran an ad
about the state of the environment. After presenting a series of
dire facts about the planet supported by images, the ad ended
with a simple admonition. "Do something, do anything!"

As I began to listen to the stories of people who had
stepped up, I began to realize that one of the greatest enemies
to creating real change is our need to have a plan before we
start to act. Without a clear plan for success, we often stay on
the sidelines. We may sit around for years waiting for the perfect path to appear, when what we really need to do is to start.
The best advice for those who want to change things is simply to get started, to do something, anything. As mystic Kabir
once wrote, "Wherever you are is the entry point."

One of the most powerful steps we can take is to get people together to start talking about how we want the future to
be different. A case in point is the story of how a priest and a
small group of citizens transformed one of the worst slums in
the world.

Transforming the Most Violent Place on Earth

In 1996 the United Nations issued a statement naming Jardim Ângela, a slum district in São Paulo, Brazil, as one of the most violent places on earth. Jardim Ângela and two other districts, Capão Redondo and Jardim São Luis, were considered by the São Paulo Civil Police to be the *triangle of death.* The district of three-hundred thousand residents had a murder rate higher than in most war zones, with 538 murders in 1996 alone and most of the victims being teenagers. Police presence in the district consisted mostly of night raids by heavily armed police platoons focused on drug crime. The schools, the community, and its youth were trapped in a cycle of violence and hopelessness.

Father Jaime Crowe was an Irish priest who had lived in the district for almost a decade and had witnessed the cycle of hopelessness build. According to a report in the September 25, 2010, edition of the *Globe and Mail,* Father Crowe said, "There wasn't a day that would go by when I walked around the parish that I wouldn't step across two or three bodies. To step over a body in front of a door with a newspaper over it to have a drink, people would think nothing of it. Children, small children, would tell me that life was not worth living."

There often comes a moment when people have simply had enough, a moment when someone realizes that he must get started, even without a coherent plan to fix the problem. That is, a person decides to act even before she knows what steps she must take to succeed.

For Father Crowe that first step came when he organized a march on November 2, 1996, to the cemetery where many of the community's murder victims, mostly teens, were buried. Five thousand people walked in that March for Peace and Life. That same year, Father Crowe and other community leaders began a weekly meeting they called the Forum for the Defense of Life. The forum brought together community leaders, police officials, and school officials. The idea behind the meetings was to generate ideas on how to solve the neighborhood's many challenges. In the beginning all they could do was talk, but talking is often a powerful precursor to creating change.

As word spread about the group's weekly meetings, international aid agencies and municipal leaders started attending and were soon joined by hundreds of local residents. During these weekly meetings, ideas on how to end the violence began to surface along with a growing resolve to put them into action. One early realization that emerged from these meetings was that doing something about schools was critical. The schools in the slum were dangerous and offered only very basic education, often for only four hours a day, so there was little hope of upward mobility for the youth. Many children dropped out and began dealing drugs by the age of twelve or thirteen.

The focus on revitalizing the schools soon began to bear fruit. Classrooms started to fill, not only with young students but also with adults and teenagers who wanted a better life. Another focus was policing. It became obvious that residents feared the police almost as much as they feared the gangs. Many police officers had been implicated in thousands of contract slayings in the slums of São Paulo. Residents wanted the police integrated into the community rather than behaving like an enemy force. Even former strong-arm police leaders began to attend the meetings and were captivated by the ideas the community was generating. In 1998, after two years of pressure from the forum meetings, the police opened a station in the district and began the practice of community policing.

The results of these forum meetings were not instantaneous. In 1996 there were 538 murders, but the murder rate peaked in 2001, five years later. Finally, in 2002, the district began to see a reduction in homicides that continued to tick down with each passing year: 254 in 2002, 212 in 2003, 172 in 2004, 119 in 2005, and only 91 in 2006. Do the math: that is an 83 percent reduction in murders. More importantly, a vibrant community emerged from the process. The March for Peace and Life still happens every year, and the weekly meetings still take place. The march has grown from five thousand to twenty-five thousand participants. This trend to violence reduction has stood the test of time through 2019.

The point of this story is that stepping up often means getting people together to talk about the future. There is no need for a perfect plan or to even know where the process will lead. What is needed is a desire to create change and the intention to gain allies to make that change happen. The story of Father Jaime Crowe and the renewal of Jardim Ângela have been written up in numerous journals and newspapers around the world. A quick internet search using his name will give the reader lots of information. The book *Arrival City* by Doug Saunders (Knopf Canada, 2010) also featured the story.

How a Small Group of Frontline People Turned a Hospital Around

Of course, most of us are not trying to transform a slum where murders are a daily part of life. We may be in a school where a culture of disrespect and bullying have become the norm, we may live in a neighborhood where litter has become commonplace, we may be in a workplace where life-work balance has become the butt of jokes or in an organization where poor service and poor morale are an accepted reality. Regardless of the challenge, the principle of doing something—of just getting started—is critical.

I have discovered that part of *doing something* almost always begins with people getting together and talking about the future. Almost always there is a need for someone to start that process.

Take the case of Mercy Hospital in Sioux City, Iowa. The hospital had a long history of serving its community, but by the time Peter Makowski arrived as the new CEO, the hospital's reputation had been tarnished. Service and morale at the hospital had deteriorated, relationships with the physician community were at a low point, and the word on the street was, "If you are really sick, go to Mercy, but if you want to be cared for in a compassionate way, go somewhere else." The hospital was losing market share, and staff often commented that as they walked through the corridors of Mercy they saw few friendly or happy faces. Although the hospital still provided great quality care, people told Makowski that the "spirit of Mercy" was missing in action.

Transforming an organization with poor morale and service back to its former glory may seem like a radically different challenge than creating hope in the most violent place on earth, but in both cases the act of stepping up involved people gathering to talk about a different future with no clear plan of how they would create it. Makowski began meeting with his leadership team and sharing his vision of a better future for Mercy. For months they met and talked about what they wanted and what was required to turn the hospital around.

Yet one of the most important steps in the hospital's transformation had nothing to do with the people who had leader roles printed on their business cards. A group of frontline employees asked the CEO if they could meet weekly, often on their own time. The group called itself the respiriting committee. Like those residents at the Forum for the Defense of Life in São Paulo, these people had no idea how to make the changes they wanted. What they did know, however, was that they were tired of the low morale, poor service, and unhappy faces, and they wanted change. They were also naïve enough to think they could do something about it and decided it was 100 percent their responsibility to do something about it.

For a year they met and shared ideas. Many of the employees took the inherent personal risks involved in stepping up. They bore the potential scorn of those coworkers who felt they were kissing up with management, and they felt at risk by speaking up about managers who were hindering creation of a more positive work environment. Stories began to emerge about the way many of these frontline people were regularly challenging the bad attitudes of peers as they called on their coworkers to stop the negativity and choose their attitude.

Ultimately, the respiriting committee came up with the idea for a campaign to win staff back by challenging them with four simple principles, including *choose your attitude* and *make someone's day*. Within a few short years, staff engagement scores shot up, market share grew, the hospital won quality awards, and, most of all, people in the community began to make unsolicited comments about the new spirit they saw at Mercy Hospital.

On one hand, this is just another story about a CEO and a new management team that came in and turned an organization around. But at a deeper level, it is the story of individuals who chose to step up even before they had a clear plan for change. It is the story of a small group of committed frontline employees who risked ridicule to advocate for change. It is the story of a few managers who joined Makowski in confronting the prevailing gloom that had overtaken the hospital. It is the story of what happens when people come together and start talking about a different future.

Doing Something in Action

Imagine the power of this simple idea: do something, do anything!

Any student in a school where bullying is the norm today could start a forum for the defense of school spirit. He or she could start meeting and let the ideas flow. Any manager or associate in a company could start having conversations with a few colleagues about how to achieve a better work-life balance within the organization. Even without a clear plan or some official sanction from management, he or she could just start taking some actions to create more balance. A few neighbors could gather and begin to talk about how to clean up the neighborhood.

Think about this for a moment: everything that has *ever* been accomplished began with someone taking a single step. Almost nothing ever accomplished had a detailed plan at the beginning, and even if it did, the path to success likely had little resemblance to that initial plan.

There is no guarantee that your conversations will lead to a coherent plan, but it is almost guaranteed that nothing will happen if no one begins to have the conversation. Doing something, doing anything is the key to getting started.

Let's apply *do something, do anything* to the many realms in which we might be called upon to step up. What if your marriage or romantic relationship has lost a sense of excitement and adventure? You might be tempted to wait for the perfect plan, but what if you just started? What if you began by having conversations about this aspect of your relationship, began remembering times when that sense of adventure had been present? Perhaps that conversation will lead to a few steps to get started. Maybe you on your own can start doing things like planning a surprise trip or bringing a book home and suggesting you read it together.

Perhaps you want to do something about work-life balance in your company. You are not the CEO nor a senior leader but feel strongly that work-life matters are out of balance. Why not begin by meeting with one or two allies, someone who agrees that there is a need to change? When you meet, don't focus on what someone else needs to do (remember 100/0). Instead, ask what steps you could take that might help with work-life balance.

This is exactly what happened at a real estate investment firm in the Midwest when a small group of employees began meeting on how to reclaim their lives and still get their work done. The boss did not officially sanction the group members; they simply saw that something needed to be done and decided to start.

They began with some simple ideas, such as agreeing not to email each other on weekends and trying hard not to schedule meetings after five in the evening. Soon, more employees joined the group and made the commitment to stop emailing on weekends and to work to restrict meetings to normal business hours. Over time a real shift happened in the culture because three people decided to start meeting and took a few simple steps to start. They had no idea where their efforts would lead when they started, but they wound up creating ripples everywhere. Within a year, many of their initial ideas had become official company policy!

Again, almost every accomplishment began with someone deciding to do something. It may not have been the perfect thing, but it got the ball rolling.

Think of something you would like to change right now. It could be something about your life. It could be something about your company or your community. Now, think of something you could do today to begin to create change. Think of people you could get together and begin the conversation. Imagine a forum for the defense of whatever you want to defend or a respiriting committee for whatever you want to respirit. What could you do to begin?

One last humorous example may make the point. Years ago I heard the late Richard Carlson, author of *Don't Sweat the Small Stuff*, talking about exercise. He asked the audience how many people had always wanted to exercise regularly but had never done so. To my surprise about 75 percent of the audience wanted to exercise regularly but had never been able to do it.

Carlson then said, "I want to make a suggestion that, if implemented, two weeks from now, will let you be able to say you exercise regularly. Beginning tomorrow morning when you wake up, stand by the side of your bed and do five jumping jacks. Do this for two straight weeks first thing in the day by the side of your bed, and then when someone asks if you exercise regularly you can say 'Yes, I do that first thing every morning.'"

Now I will confess that when I heard Carlson say that, my first thoughts were something like, "Give me a break, no wonder they make fun of motivational speakers!" Then I realized what he was saying. Most of us have the intention to do something but are waiting around for the perfect plan. Five jumping jacks was as good a start as anything else. Doing five jumping jacks every day would begin to change the energy. It was not enough to make someone fit, but doing something, doing anything, is often just the right way to begin stepping up.

Milo and the Plastic Straw Campaign

Over the last few years, across the globe, there has been a movement to ban or at least not to automatically provide plastic straws in restaurants. This simple practice can save millions of straws from ending up in garbage dumps, or more destructively, in the ocean. Even though I took a personal pledge to stop using straws almost fifteen years ago, I cannot take credit for the movement that has emerged.

But one fourth grader deserves an immense amount of credit. When Milo Cress was nine years old, he was at a neighborhood café, Leunig's Bistro and Café in Burlington, Vermont. He'd noticed that whenever he and his mom ordered drinks at restaurants, they automatically came with a plastic straw popped into them.

To Cress, that was odd. "It seemed like a waste to me," he told the Daily Beast. Why? He saw that a lot of patrons would take the straw out of the glass and set it aside or throw it away. And a lot of people who used straws didn't really have to.

Cress persuaded the owner to start providing a straw only when customers requested one. It not only saved money but reduced waste energy. Cress later became a crusading voice for reducing straw usage and won awards from national restaurant associations for his efforts. Today, in many cities straws have been banned and in many others are provided only on request. On a recent trip to a large resort in Costa Rica, I noticed the entire resort was straw free. While Cress may not get the direct credit, his simple choice to do something, take one single step and then another, has created waves of change for the better. Now in his late teens, he continues to be a major advocate for this issue. I love what he said in an interview with the Daily Beast: "Every time I look around, I see things that can change. I can't help but try to fix things."

Jardim Ângela began to change the night those first citizens gathered with Father Crowe to talk about the future. Mercy Hospital was on the path to respiriting itself the very first time those frontline people volunteered to put their skin in the game. The decision of three people to stop sending emails on the weekend was a first step toward greater work-life balance. Five jumping jacks won't change your life, but they're a start.

Do something—do anything. If you wait for the perfect plan, you may never step up.

Ways to Step Up

✔ **Find one thing.** Think of something at work, in your life, or in the world that you want to do something about. Instead of trying to hatch a master plan, identify one thing you can do starting immediately to move in the direction of the change you seek.

✔ **Get together.** Find a few allies and start to meet. The focus could be making your school better, improving work-life balance or morale, improving service, doing something about bullying in your school, or saving the planet. But when you meet, *don't spend one minute talking about how other people need to step up.* Instead, focus on what you can do, the steps you can take, no matter how small they may be.

✔ **Talk about the future.** Talking about the future is often a powerful precursor to significant change. Imagine how skeptical people must have been at that first meeting in that violent slum in São Paulo. If something concerns you or you want to change something, start talking together about the future.

CHAPTER 7

Always Begin in the Room You Are In

Where does change begin? It begins in this room.
Why?
Because this is the room you are in.

Peter Block

If we really want to step up and make a difference in our company and in the world we need to understand that the best place to begin stepping up is wherever you are right now. Stepping up begins when we open our eyes and see that wherever we are, whatever moment we are in, and whatever situation we find ourselves in, stepping up is available to us right there.

Remember the simple definition of stepping up I shared in the preface: "Seeing a need and deciding you are the right person to do something about it"? A corollary of this is that we must act with whatever gifts and skills we have. As Arthur Ashe, the late tennis great, once said, "To achieve greatness start where you are, use what you have, and do what you can."

Rahul Singh is a paramedic and makes his living that way. He also happens to have been named by *Time* magazine in 2010 as one of the world's one hundred most influential people. His story and how he became named by *Time* illustrate the important principle of stepping up right where you are with the skills that you have.

Rahul grew up in Montreal and Toronto, trained as a para-medic, and was working in emergency medicine. When his marriage ended in the mid-1990s, he decided to travel and wound up in southeast Nepal. While working and training at a teaching hospital, he got deployed to an area where a series of horrific mudslides had occurred.

"When I got there, it was great to be able to see the impact of your work so directly," he told me. "Every day we were get-ting clean water to people who had none, literally saving peo-ple's lives every day. We were doing really good work, and then suddenly the word came down that the agency had run out of money and they pulled the plug."

Upset about the shutdown, Rahul hiked and took a bus back to Kathmandu to find the head of the agency. The director was staying at a five-star hotel and offered to take Rahul out for a fancy steak dinner. Halfway through the meal Rahul said he felt an incredible anger well up in him: "I could hardly keep my meal down. It was such a contrast, people were living in such poverty, we were bringing clean water to people who had none, and here he was living it up. I let him have it, told him what I thought. Guess what? No surprise, he fired me!"

Rahul went back to Canada. Soon after his return, his best friend, David Gibson, died from complications of a liver trans-plant. Gibson had just married the year before and had fought like hell to stay alive. He was only in his early thirties. David's death was a deep, personal blow to Rahul, but it also became a catalyst.

"When I went to his funeral, I saw how many lives he had touched in his short life and I thought, 'Look what he did while he was here.' Then I thought, 'He's so young, and I'm not far behind, so now is the time to live.' That's when I put two and two together," Rahul said. He realized he could combine his experiences in Nepal and his training as a paramedic and make them the basis for a foundation in David's name "to meet the need for emergency medicine in the developing world."

People repeatedly have asked me this question about stepping up: what made people finally step up to take action? From my experience there are two primary drivers of stepping up, and they are both illustrated in Rahul's story. The first is anger, the feeling of having had enough, and the sense that something isn't right (and that someone has to do something about it). It was Rahul's anger—about that expensive hotel and dinner in harsh contrast to the poverty he had seen in the villages—that led him to decide that something had to be done. Anger about the slaughter of whales fueled Rex Weyler, and anger about the casual response to dead people in front of bars motivated Father Crowe.

But the second catalyst seems to be an initial sense of one's power to change things. The march to the cemetery helped Father Crowe see the potential to bring people together to advocate for change; the funeral of his friend David showed Rahul that one person could have immeasurable influence over others; and the growing number of people who attended the respiriting committee meetings at Mercy propelled group members to become bolder in confronting their colleagues.

On the back of the anger and seeing the difference his friend had made, Rahul started an organization named Global Medic and built on a simple principle: get paramedics and other emergency personnel to donate their time during emergencies, raise money for supplies, and try to get to the scene as quickly as possible. As of 2020, Global Medic has provided services in seventy-three countries, served over 3.4 million people, and responded to over two hundred global disasters. Because most of the organization's services are provided through volunteers, the impact has been significant.

Rahul has been on the scene of many of the worst disasters of the last decade, including the tsunami in Southeast Asia
and the horrific earthquake in Haiti. To this day, the charity
has only two employees, and Rahul is not one of them; he still
makes his living as a full-time paramedic.

"We have a mantra, 'The most amount of aid to the greatest number of people, for the least cost,'" Rahul told me.

He was not a fundraiser nor did he have any particular
managerial skill. What Rahul had was even more important.
He had a desire for things to be better and decided he was the
one who could do something about it. During my interview
with him, he also gave me one of the most important insights
into stepping up, a simple but profound idea: you have to use
the gifts you have to work with.

Here is what he told me: "I am a paramedic, so the natural
way for me to step up was to go do emergency medicine. For
some kid in grade 7, she might be best at holding a bake sale
to raise money. If you are a pharmaceutical company, the best
way for you to step up is providing drugs, and if you are an
airline it is about providing a plane to send the supplies. There
is a woman named Sharon who volunteers for us. She works
at a local hospital and can't take off and go to the sites. But she
comes and spends hours packing the supplies, so that's her way
of stepping up. Just because you are the one who goes to the
far-flung places doesn't make you more important. Each of us
has to step up with what we have to offer."

Begin Where You Are, Do What You Can

Beginning where you are and doing what you can with your
unique set of skills is critical. A few years ago my partner,
Janice, and I made a trip to Uganda where we spent about

five weeks doing pro bono work for an organization that has helped thousands of women raise themselves out of poverty. When we returned home we experienced a bit of a funk, as we were back at home without that deep sense of purpose that we had every day in Uganda. Then one day we stopped at a stoplight where a homeless man was begging for money. He looked as poor and as dejected as many of those we had seen in Uganda.

"What a shame we had to go all that way to Uganda to help people," Janice said. "We should do something right here where we live."

Often, we think we have to go to some distant place to step up when the opportunity is sitting right in front of us. Over the next several months, with our eyes open now, we started noticing the punishing poverty and hopelessness within blocks of our home. We adopted a homeless man by becoming his main supplier for recyclable products that he could take for refunds. I offered my consulting services for free to an organization four blocks from my home that does extensive work with homeless people and wound up joining the board.

Sometimes to step up we must put aside visions of some larger work to start acting right where we are now. A young man in his early twenties wrote an email to Rex Weyler after reading about how he and others had helped stop the whale hunt. Attracted to the sense of adventure and purpose in the whale campaign, the young idealist told Weyler that he wanted to do something big like that and help save the planet. Rex wrote him back, saying that it was great to want to do something big, but that he should start by finding something he could do right in his own neighborhood.

At first the young man seemed discouraged by the idea, but some months later the young man wrote back. After receiving the advice to look in his own backyard, he noticed that on recycling day, few houses in his neighborhood recycled very much. So he put together a simple flier showing what a difference recycling makes, he went out and got scores of blue bins, and then he went door to door to win his neighbors to recycling. By the end of just a few weeks' work, almost every house in his neighborhood had full blue boxes outside. He stepped up right where he was with the gifts he had. Most of all, he realized that stepping up right where he was planted had produced immediate results.

Stepping Up Is about Seeing the Possible in the Mundane

Many forms of stepping up featured in this book were written on the larger landscape. Divisions of companies turned into profit engines, whale hunts stopped, school systems transformed, and violent slums turned into vibrant communities. But much of stepping up is about seeing the possible in what may seem mundane.

Based in Canada, WestJet is one of the most profitable airlines in the world. Over its twenty-six-year history the company has gobbled up market share from its competitors, mostly because of an intense focus on great customer service. Almost any job offers the possibility of stepping up and making a difference. All that is required is that we keep our eyes open, as WestJet illustrates.

An agent at one of WestJet's call centers received a call one day from a distraught father. His adult daughter had just had a cardiac arrest. She had been admitted to a hospital with a virus in her heart, and there was a reasonable chance she would not make it. The parents needed to catch a flight as soon as possible, as it might be their last chance to see their daughter alive. The agent told them a flight was leaving in just a few minutes and another flight was not scheduled for some time. She easily could have offered her regrets and wished them well. Instead, she got them two tickets for the flight that was about to leave and told them to head to the airport immediately. Then she stepped up.

She contacted the duty manager at the airport and worked through two gate agents to convince them to delay the plane. They held the plane at the gate, and it left the moment the parents boarded. The agent could have sold them tickets for the next flight, but if she had, she would have missed the opportunity to make a difference right there in that moment. Instead, she stepped up—she made a difference for these parents, she enhanced the reputation of WestJet, and she probably inspired others as well.

Sometimes stepping up can mean simply keeping your eyes open and asking, "How might I make a difference now, right here where I am?" Stepping up is asking the question that the elderly store owner asked Howard Behar: "If not me, then who?" You see, part of stepping up is realizing at any moment that if you don't step up, maybe no one will do so. Maybe your stepping up means more than you can ever imagine.

That's what happened when a taxi driver named Rajbir Singh picked up a ninety-two-year-old woman in Roseville, California, in February 2020. The woman told him she needed to go to the bank to withdraw $25,000 to settle a debt with the Internal Revenue Service. Singh tried to convince her that it was likely a scam, but the woman insisted on going to the bank. Singh could easily have just let it go, but he went out of his way to take her to a local police station and then asked officers to talk to her. The police were able to convince her that she should ignore the scammers.

Saving a Stranger on a Bus

Years ago, a young woman from Toronto named Sameera told me one of the most profound stories I have ever heard. After a visit to her city, her parents boarded a flight for home, but her mother died suddenly of a cardiac episode during the flight. Days later, Sameera found herself sitting in a funeral home during calling hours, and she did not know many of the visitors. She kept asking her father and her brothers who each person was, but no one knew one woman sitting in a corner.

The daughter went to the middle-aged woman and engaged her in conversation. "I am her only daughter," she said, "and my family and I were just talking about the fact that none of us know you. So I am wondering, how did you know my mother?"

The woman paused and then replied, "I am sorry to say, I did not know your mother."

Taken aback, the daughter said, "I don't understand. Then why are you here?"

"Well it is a bit of a long story," the woman began.

She continued: "About five years ago I was going through a very, very difficult time in my life. I was so distraught that I had made a plan to kill myself. That day I was riding a bus, sitting next to a woman who was very engrossed in a book. Halfway through the trip she put her book down on her lap and turned to me saying, 'You look like a woman who needs to talk.'

"For the rest of the bus ride, I don't know why, I confided in her. She talked to me. She told me that sometimes things seem so dark but that if we hold on, the light comes. When I got home I changed my mind. I decided to live.

"I was so into myself that day I never even asked what her name was, but then three days ago I saw her picture in the paper. You see, I did not know your mother. I did not even know her name, but her twenty minutes with me saved my life. So I came to say thank you."

During the normal routine of riding a bus, Sameera's mother had stepped up. She had felt a need and thought, "Maybe I can do something about it." She just as easily could have kept her nose in the book or minded her own business. She might have said, "Let someone else clean this up later." Instead, she said, "If not me, who? If not now, when?" Of course not every step up will have such a significant consequence, but this is the point too. We step up not knowing the consequences.

What Is the Role You Can Best Play?

Here are some questions to ask yourself: What is something you care deeply about? What role are you best positioned to play in solving that problem?

To make a difference we must often get ego out of the way. Doing something big is nice, but doing something big is almost always an outgrowth of doing something smaller. Rahul did not set out to be one of *Time's* most influential people. He saw a need and connected it with his skill as a paramedic.

What can you do right now where you are? How can you step up and make your company better, perhaps in its morale, its reputation, its service? How can you step up and make your community better?

Maybe you won't stop poverty or solve world hunger, but there probably is a homeless person within a few blocks of your home or a dissatisfied customer on the other side of your desk.

Heartbreak and Hope in Haiti

Rahul Singh, like so many people who have stepped up, wondered aloud to me if he has done enough: "I think I have not stepped up enough. Why are we only bringing in a million dollars a year when the need is so great?"

When the Haiti earthquake occurred, Global Medic aid was among the first to arrive. Volunteers flew into the Dominican Republic and drove across the border into Haiti, arriving on the scene a mere sixty hours after the quake. They would be in Haiti for four months. For every life they saved there were disappointments. Rahul told me heartwarming and heartbreaking stories of what it is like to be on the front lines of such a disaster. One story stood out. This is the story in his words:

"I had a moment when I wanted to throw up my hands and say this is not worth it. I was working from five in the morning until late at night. I had not even slept the night before when a guy with a shotgun taps me on the shoulder and tells me there is a woman whose children were sick. She had triplets three days before the quake. One died during the quake and the other two were sick. It was 5:30 Sunday morning, and the sun had just come up.

"The only facility for an eight-day-old infant was run by the Israelis some twenty kilometers away. At day six in Haiti, it might as well have been two thousand miles away! The streets were not safe, and there were looters everywhere and people with guns. I was going to say no but something in me could not do it. We packed her up with her two infants in a Land Cruiser and headed that way. At one point the car was surrounded by such a large mob that the driver had to shoot a few rounds out the window to clear the crowd.

"All the time as we drove, and it took most of the day, I was working on the kid. At one point during the drive I realized he had died. In Toronto where I live the police would have come and guided us to the hospital. But here, it was simply too far and had taken too long. I did not have the heart to tell her he was dead so I bundled him up tightly and handed him back to her. She cuddled him in her arms until we arrived at the makeshift hospital.

"When we finally arrived, the Israelis took the one kid in right away and then they told me I needed to tell the mom that the other one was dead and ask her if she wanted to bury him. So I told her that her son was dead. It was so odd. At home we would have to fill out certificates of death and all kinds of paperwork. But here there would be no record of this boy's death; there were simply too many to keep count. I was angry for even going and wondered how many people did not get drinking water that day because I came here with these kids.

"But that day, when I got back to our base, some of the kids led a cheer in Creole about how we had saved the day for them and given them hope. Then I thought, 'Look what they are going through, and they have hope. Who am I to be pissed?'"

In the months they were there, Global Medic served seven thousand patients, brought in millions of dollars in meds, and distributed a million liters of fresh water every week. Even if you step up, you can't fix everything.

Of course it was anger in part that had motivated Rahul in the first place, anger at that steak dinner at the five-star hotel and then the death of his best friend. I asked him what he would say to others about stepping up.

"There is a sense of urgency," he said. "Life is short; if you are not going to step up now, then when will you? You don't want to look back on your life and wish you had stepped up and changed something."

Ways to Step Up

✔ **Identify your skills.** What skill do you have for stepping up? Think of how you can apply that skill toward something you care about. Maybe you can speak in front of groups, maybe you write well, or maybe your main gift is time. How can you use what you have right now to make a difference?

✔ **Think about your average day at work or in your life.** What are all the ways you could step up and make a bigger difference in your daily life without moving anywhere or changing anything except the way you see your job or role?

CHAPTER 8

Leadership Is Not a Position

If your actions inspire others to dream more,
learn more, do more, and become more, you are
a leader.

John Quincy Adams

Leadership is not a position. You can't be assigned or appointed to be a leader. Leadership is not about what your business card says, what your title is, or where you sit on the organizational chart in your company. Leadership is a posture; it is a decision that you want to have influence over others in a positive way.

The Day They Stood Up to the Bullies

David Shepherd and Travis Price did not hold positions of leadership, but in September 2007 they decided to lead. It was a normal first week of school at Central Kings Rural High School in Nova Scotia, Canada, when a student arrived at school wearing a pink polo shirt. Chuck McNeill was a ninth grader, and it was his first day at the school, having just moved to the community. It turned out not to be a very good day. He was bullied mercilessly by a group of twelfth graders who called him gay and told him that if he ever wore a pink shirt again, they would beat him to a pulp. Welcome to the school!

Events like this happen every day in schools around the world, often with grave consequences as evidenced by recent events such as the suicide of a Rutgers University student in New Jersey. According to the Centers for Disease Control, over 4,400 teens commit suicide every year in the United States alone, and students who are bullied are up to nine times more likely to take their life than those who are not bullied. One in four American youth will be bullied during their adolescence, and it usually becomes an ongoing problem after the first incident. A British study suggests that half of teen suicides are related to bullying. That means as many as 2,200 teens may commit suicide in the United States every year because of bullying! According to a report by ABC News, some 160,000 US students stay home every day out of fear of bullying! (That's just one of the many statistics available on bullying. Some cited in this book come from http://www.bullyingstatistics.org/content/bullying-and -suicide.html.)

At Central Kings High, twelfth graders David Shepherd and Travis Price heard about the bullying incident and decided to act. David later said, "I just figured enough is enough. I figured this had gone too far, someone needs to do something about it. I told Travis we should be the ones to do something, and he agreed." David and Travis were interviewed a few days later on national television, and the story was reported on CBC. You can read the interview at http://www.cbc.ca/news/canada /nova-scotia/story/2007/09/18/pink-tshirts-students.html.

They hatched a simple idea: they would go to a local discount store and purchase as many pink T-shirts and tank tops as they could find. Through Facebook and email later that night, they tried to get as many people as possible to agree to join what they had dubbed a "sea of pink." The next morning, not only did students don the fifty shirts and tank tops David and Travis bought. Almost eight hundred of the one thousand students at the school wore some kind of pink. The boys were overwhelmed with the response.

One of the bullies saw the sea of pink and threw a trash-can in anger, but as David said later, "Not a peep was heard from the bullies after that day." The story was picked up by the national media across Canada and later overseas. Within a week schools across Nova Scotia were wearing pink, the next week schools across Canada joined in, and within a month schools in other countries started doing so.

Over a decade later the "pink shirt day" movement has spread across the globe and in 2012 the United Nations declared May 4 as Anti-Bullying day. Schools across Canada and elsewhere hold annual pink shirt days, all because two twelfth graders decided to step up and lead. No one appointed them, they were not the chairs of (or even members of) an anti-bullying committee, and they were not the stars of the football team. They simply decided to be leaders. David told CBC News, "We won't be able to stop all bullying, but if enough of us step up and just do what we can, we can get rid of most of it." See www.pinkshirtday.ca for more information about the annual event.

You Can't Not Lead

Not only is leadership not a position, but the truth also is that you can't *not* lead. That is, whether you want to or not, you are influencing others. Simply by showing up a certain way in our life and work, each of us creates a ripple even if we don't intend to.

Try this little experiment. Next time you enter a conversation that is negative, intentionally shift gears and watch what happens. If someone is talking negatively about your company or a coworker or a mutual acquaintance, turn it around and make a positive comment. Watch how the energy shifts. In fact, by saying nothing we are actually taking a leading role without choosing to do so. That is why bullying experts talk about bystanders being a critical element of bullying culture in work or school. Doing nothing thus is a form of leading.

Or try one day to have no influence at all. Simply be quiet on every issue that comes up. Before you know it, people will be pressing you for your viewpoint. Your very silence and desire to have no influence in fact will have influenced the course of the conversation. Remember back to our earlier conversation about yawning; whatever we do causes a reaction.

As parents, we should be acutely aware of how we lead even when we are not trying. Think about those times you suddenly find yourself sounding like your mother or father, even though you said you'd never do that. They were influencing you even when they did not know it.

Since leadership is not a position, it means that each of us can throw punches far above our weight class. We don't need a title or a position of power to have influence. Of course, claiming we have no influence is a great crutch that can keep us from having to step up. We can say things like, "If they ever give me some real authority around here, let me tell you what I would do." Well, here is a news flash—you already have authority. You already are a leader. The only question is how are you using the influence that you already have?

One way to get in touch with how you want to be influential is to ask yourself what your intention is every day. That is, in what way do you want to influence others every day, just by the way you show up? Over the years in workshop sessions I have led, I have asked thousands of people to do a simple exercise of stating how they intend to influence others every day. I am always both amazed and inspired by the answers people give. A receptionist in a law firm, for example, told me that her intention was that every person who met her all day long got a "shot of friendliness" so that people felt the world was a friendlier place because they encountered her. The list of intentions is inspiring. Some say they want to bring kindness, others goodness, compassion, energy, courage, or hope. Your position does not limit the way you can influence others. This woman was "only" a receptionist, but she could influence others in a profound way by holding that intention.

What is your intention every day? How do you want to influence others by the way you show up?

The Story behind the Starbucks Frappuccino

Part of stepping up is deciding to lead bigger than the pre-scribed formal role you have. Your job description may say you have a certain responsibility, but if you want to get ahead, decide to lead bigger than your role says you should.

Here are some of my favorite examples. You probably have had a Starbucks Frappuccino, and you may have guessed that the Frappuccino had a huge impact on Starbucks' profit growth. What you probably don't know is the story behind the drink.

According to Howard Behar, former president of Starbucks International, the Frappuccino almost never got launched. It was the summer of 1993 in Santa Monica, California, when frontline team members noticed that some local coffee shops were selling iced dessert coffee drinks, which was taking away customers from the local Starbucks stores. Some front-line staff members and the local manager felt they needed to get some blenders and create a drink to compete with the local business. Dina Campion, the manager of the stores in the Los Angeles area, gave Behar, her boss, a taste of the drink, and said that about thirty people every day were asking for the dessert drinks.

According to Behar, he floated the idea up to the senior team at Starbucks. Although executives liked the drink, Behar says, "The marketing manager who was in charge of product innovations said we were in the hot coffee business so he thought it was not the right product. The final vote was seven to one against." Behar delivered the bad news to Campion and her team. In most cases that would have been the end of the story, but Behar says, "Dina was like a little dog with sharp teeth. She stayed on me, kept calling me, and then finally went ahead and started serving the drinks anyway."

The perseverance of Dina and her frontline team would wind up leading to one of the most successful products in modern business history. It was not in the store manager's job description to come up with new products. In fact, Starbucks had a group of people whose job was to create new menu items. But the folks in Santa Monica kept bugging Behar, then vice president at Starbucks. They kept pushing, saying this idea was a winner, even when the answer came back as no. They started experimenting anyway. Within a few months, sales of the new drinks skyrocketed. The perseverance paid off, and the cold drinks became a major product for Starbucks, in part because a few people led in an area where they were not supposed to be leaders. They did not let position get in the way of choosing to lead. That's the way Howard Behar told me the story. Even though the exact details may depend on whom you ask, the one thing for certain is that the folks in Santa Monica had a big impact on the company.

The Frappuccino changed the trajectory of the company by bringing in new customers who were not normally coffee drinkers and filling its stores in the afternoon and during warm weather when the coffee business was typically slow. The Frappuccino accounted for 11 percent of the company's summer sales and helped push Starbucks stock to an all-time high.

How a Call Center Agent Won a Customer for Life

Leading beyond your defined role can happen in the most unlikely of places. Canadian Tire is a large, home-grown retail hardware and general goods chain. Some years ago the company leaders came up with a slogan: *Customers for Life*. They wanted to be so service-oriented and treat customers so well that they would become customers for a lifetime.

In some jobs it was pretty obvious how people could take the lead on this effort. But the connection was not so evident for one group of people, employees in a call center who spent their entire day calling people whose store-sponsored credit cards were overdue. All day long they called delinquent customers to try to get them to pay their bills. It sounds like a tough way to win customers for life. In fact, who wants customers for life who can't pay their bills? It would be easy to cut some slack for anyone in that department who thought, "It's not my job to win customers for life!"

One agent made an outgoing call to talk to a woman who was months behind on paying a fairly substantial bill to Canadian Tire. The agent asked when the money might be paid, and the woman told her a story. She said that she had decided some time earlier to start a home candle-making business in which she would have parties at people's houses to sell her candles. She had bought a large amount of supplies at Canadian Tire to start the business, but there was one big wrinkle in her plan: she could not get people to host the parties. The woman apologized for not being able to pay her bill but said that she had no idea when she could pay, given the large amount of supplies she had on hand and with little prospect for parties.

Most of the time this is where the story would end. The agent would say she was sorry to hear about the woman's plight and then admonish her to pay very soon. The agent might have even told a few people the story. She could easily be forgiven for not trying to win a customer for life. But few agents would have done what she did.

The next day she called the woman up and said, "I have been thinking about your situation, and I have an idea. We have several hundred people, mostly women, who work here at the call center. I'd like to organize a day where we have some candle parties during lunch times here at the center. I will put up fliers, talk up the party, and all you need to do is show up with your candles."

A few weeks later they held the parties. Not only did the woman sell out most of her inventory, but many of the agents also said they'd like to hold parties in their homes. The day of parties at the call center launched the struggling business. The woman paid off her credit card and a year later sent a letter to the president of Canadian Tire about what a difference this agent had made in her life and business. The agent won an award from the company. She had, of course, won a customer for life.

This simple story—told to me by Brigid Pelino, a former Canadian Tire executive now at Economical Insurance—illustrates many of the points in this book. First is the issue of responsibility; it was not in the agent's job description to help people pay their bills or to help struggling businesses become successful, but she took responsibility anyway. She could have easily said "that's not my job" to do that. Instead, she did what everyone does who steps up; she saw a need and decided she was the right person to do something about it. This is what 100 percent responsibility means in action. It means saying "Why not me?" instead of "Why me?"

It also illustrates the profound difference we can make regardless of where we sit. Stepping up is about doing what you can, where you are, and with what you have. Many of us are waiting to be in a position of influence before we influence, when the opposite is more representative of reality: the more we influence, the more we will be given the formal opportunity to influence in a more significant role. That agent's credibility in the company grew because she decided to lead. Awards are not given to those who simply carry their weight but to those who decide to lead in a way greater than their position.

Leading beyond Our Position Changes Us

The choice to lead beyond our position changes us and changes the organizations we are part of. David and Travis remain involved in tackling bullying globally, and one of them almost became the youngest provincial legislature member in history in Nova Scotia. Howard Behar, who ran seventy stores for Starbucks, would later be put in charge of the entire international operation of Starbucks (and folks at the company still talk about "Howard Squared" to indicate the impact Howard Schultz and Howard Behar had on Starbucks' success). Dina Campion would later move into a senior role at Starbucks. The bottom line is that when we lead beyond our position, we become influential in ways we never imagined.

Stepping up is about taking a position of leadership even if no one is asking you to do it. That is what David and Travis did in September 2007 when they took on bullying. That is what those committed few did at Starbucks when they fought for the cold coffee drinks. It's what the agent did at Canadian Tire when she stepped out of her role to help a delinquent credit card holder.

You are leading right now, whatever your position may be. Why not lead bigger than your position?

Ways to Step Up

✔ **State your intention.** Write down how you want to change the world or your workplace (or family) every day. Write that intention on a card. Carry it with you. Your intention might be compassion, it might be respect, it might be optimism or energy. Whatever it is, look for ways to influence in the direction of that intention all day long.

✔ **Punch above your weight or formal position.** Come up with ideas for new products and innovations even if it's not in your job description. Win customers for life even if it's not your department, and generally go bigger than whatever your role says you *must* do.

✔ **Don't let your lack of position get in the way of your influence.** David and Travis had no position, but they did lead. How could you lead right now even though you have no position?

CHAPTER 9

Stepping Up by Speaking Up

The world is waiting to hear your voice.

Sometimes, just speaking is a form of stepping up and often one of great consequence. That is, the act of bringing up an idea that may be unpopular or challenging the status quo with your words is a powerful form of stepping up. Josh Blair, a former executive vice president at TELUS, put it this way: "Stepping up is often about having the courage to go to an uninvited place." That uninvited place could be challenging your company, giving feedback to a colleague or friend, or breaking the silence to speak up for something you believe in.

The idea of stepping up and speaking up in an uninvited way brings fear to most of us. In our personal lives we fear that we might damage our relationships with friends, colleagues, or family members by speaking an unpopular truth. The prospect of speaking up seems even more daunting in the workplace, where we all know that kissing up and getting with the program is the path to success, no?

I do not pretend that speaking up involves no risk. Whistleblowers are often ostracized, friends and colleagues don't always want to hear feedback (even if it will help them), and at some workplaces speaking up is neither rewarded nor welcome. Yet it also must be noted that those who do speak up often have a profound influence on others and on their organizations, while failure to speak up can have devastating effects on a society, a company, or a life.

The Myth of Kissing Up

Let's begin by exploring a popularly held myth that in the world of work, those who kiss up and keep silent are more likely to get ahead. When I interviewed senior executives and CEOs for this book, I asked them this question: how do you feel about people who speak up and challenge things? To a person, they all talked about how valuable such people are, how much they improve the organization, and how little they admire yes people. Of course, many bosses really do want to be surrounded by people who won't challenge things, but my experience has been that this attitude is not the norm.

One clue to unraveling this myth can be found in the work of the late Dr. Dominic Infante and Dr. William Gorden, two retired professors of communication studies at Kent State University in Ohio. I owe Dr. Infante a personal debt of gratitude because he directed my doctoral dissertation and will be forever one of my favorite people. That's because during the oral defense of my competency exams, he asked, "Would you like a hint?" when he saw that I had no clue as to the answer to an important question. A rather hard-nosed colleague scornfully looked at him and said, "A hint." Dr. Infante merely smiled and said, "Yes, a hint," and proceeded to give me a big hint.

Dr. Infante spent a good deal of his career studying two constructs called *argumentativeness* and *verbal aggression*. Simply put, people who are high in argumentativeness like a good debate, tend to speak up with their ideas, and challenge things. Verbal aggressiveness has to do with finger-pointing and blaming, people who tend to use a great deal of *you* language and often put down others with their communication. Years of research by Dr. Infante showed that managers routinely rated employees much higher who were high in argumentativeness. Ironically, those most likely to speak up were rated highest, not lowest. On the other hand, those who were high in verbal aggression were consistently rated the lowest by managers. Perhaps surprisingly, research has shown that argumentative people actually have better marriages but being verbally aggressive won't help your love life.

In fact, Dr. Infante did a whole series of research studies and journal articles on argumentativeness, and many of these can be accessed on the internet. My dissertation explored similar themes, and I discovered that not only are those who speak up rated more highly at work but that employees also are more committed and engaged in workplaces where speaking up is encouraged. Employees deemed low in argumentativeness were actually rated lower by their supervisors, so argue away, keeping in mind one huge caveat: not all workplaces or all managers want someone to speak up. So beware, or, better yet, find another boss if yours prefers silence.

The moral of the story is simple. People who step up and challenge things are actually more likely to get ahead, but only if they do so in a way that is not perceived as finger-pointing and blaming. If you believe that all your complaining over the years was a form of stepping up, I beg to differ. Complaining, usually characterized by lots of *you* and *they* language, is a mask for *not* stepping up. Like verbally aggressive people, complainers are neither respected nor promoted.

Speaking up in a positive way means challenging things but focusing on what we all need to do to make things better. Here is a surefire way to know whether you are speaking up or complaining: If your talk frequently uses the words *you* and *they,* you are probably complaining. If you are using lots of *I* and *we,* you are probably speaking up in a positive way.

The Power of Breaking the Silence

Stepping up by speaking up can have real, positive effects both for your company and your career. At one of my large clients, friends and colleagues often approached a woman who worked in benefits about a problem with the services of her company. Talking to other colleagues, she realized that this was a common occurrence and that her fellow managers and employees often felt powerless to solve customer complaints that came to them directly. Even though it was not her area of responsibility, she chose to speak up at a company town hall meeting. She suggested that the company needed a method for all employees to get issues resolved when customers brought them directly to the employees, something better than suggesting the customers call customer service. She said that this inability to act was bad for the brand and left employees feeling powerless. It was a bit of a risk, speaking up and raising what could be an unpopular issue.

Yet her speaking up encouraged two other leaders to step up. Those two leaders spearheaded an effort to create a problem resolution system where a customer issue brought to the company by an employee or manager could be resolved in forty-eight hours. The system was implemented and became a great success but likely would never have happened if this one woman had not spoken up at a town hall meeting about an issue far from her area of responsibility. She did not say *you* need to fix this, she said *we* need to fix this.

Breaking the silence is an important kind of stepping up, a willingness to say what everyone is thinking but no one seems willing to say. It is no accident that in the monarchies of the past, the court jester was a very powerful position because the jester could often say things that everyone else was thinking but no one else dared say (hence the well-known saying "there's many a true word spoken in jest").

Being the one who breaks the silence can be nerve racking, yet this kind of stepping up is often critical. In one of my client companies there was a gathering of middle and senior leaders. Over the preceding year, as the company grappled with a recession, senior leaders had become tighter and tighter about controlling expenses, often leading to micromanagement by leaders throughout the organization.

The word on the street was that middle managers did not feel trusted. Many felt that the senior people needed to tell middle managers what needed to be done and trust their judgment to do so, instead of tying their hands with procedures. At this gathering, managers were dancing around the issue until one manager raised his hand.

"Look," he said, "no one seems willing to say it, but the real problem is that you guys are acting like control freaks." You could hear a pin drop. He had said what probably everyone in the room was thinking, but he had actually said it! In fairness, he had used some *you* language, but he had done so in a very constructive way. He went on to say, "We need you to trust us and hold us accountable, then we need to step up and prove we deserve it."

His speaking up created some helpful dialogue in the moment, but there was also nervousness and defensiveness. As when Jerry McGuire (the character in the movie of the same name) put his mission statement in colleagues' inboxes, people cheered outwardly, but some wondered if he would pay a price for speaking up. What happened later at my client's is most instructive.

One of the senior leaders who had been named a control freak by this man told me that he got to thinking later that night about what the manager had said. As the financial crisis abated, the CEO had let loose some of the controls on the senior team, but the senior team had not done the same with its people. He realized that the manager who spoke up was correct; these leaders were acting like control freaks. His speaking up helped loosen the controls, and that senior manager told the story over and over again for the next year. This stepping up story became folklore and a catalyst for positive change across the company

Stepping up by speaking up can mean defending someone at school when others are making fun of him, it can be challenging the scheduling of an after-hours meeting in a company where work-life balance is out of control, it can mean being the one who says, "Let's have the gossip stop here instead of spreading it," and it can often simply mean a willingness to be unpopular in the moment just because it is the right thing to do. In the age of Me Too, it could mean confronting a sexist comment and speaking up to call out inappropriate behavior.

If You Don't Have Something Nice to Say

My mother is a native New Yorker although Canadian by descent. Her family raised her to be polite and speak only when you have something nice to say. But if you want to step up and make a difference, there are times when you have to speak up, even if it may not be popular.

A few years ago my mother was sitting at lunch with a group of colleagues, including a young coworker who had just moved back into her parents' home after living with a boyfriend for two years. The young woman was complaining about how controlling her dad was and how, after being on her own for two years, she resented being told when to go home and being asked where she was going. The situation had gotten so bad that her mother and father were no longer speaking to each other as they disagreed on how to handle the conflict with their daughter.

The rest of the lunchroom gang listened and lent support, even though in her absence they remarked that she was, after all, at her parents' house. My mother listened to the daily rant but finally had enough and decided to speak up. She did not do it to look good or to show up her young colleague. She said, "Look, I have to say you have some nerve. You move out and then move back into your parents' house. You are living off of them, and now you resent that they want some say? For God's sake, now your mother and father are not even talking to each other! Do you think that is right? Maybe you'd better look at yourself." My mother left the table.

A week later, the young colleague came to my mother. "Irene, I have to tell you that it bothered me when you said what you said at lunch last week," the young woman remarked. "But later that day, I started thinking about what you said. I went to my father and apologized, and we have worked things out. My mother and father are talking again. Thanks for saying what you said."

Speaking up can also take the form of challenging our colleagues to do better. Years ago, I was staying at a Ritz-Carlton outside of Atlanta, Georgia. The hotel chain is known for having great customer service, and I was standing at the front desk receiving that great service from a young front desk associate. While she was helping me, another guest came up to the front desk where two Ritz employees were talking to each other about a ballgame they had seen the night before. They continued talking as the guest waited to be served. The young woman serving me turned her head ever

so gently keeping her eyes on me and whispered to her colleagues, "There is a guest present." Immediately they ceased
talking and turned their attention to the guest. It was subtle
but immensely profound.

The woman at the front desk had stepped up. She had
broken a code of silence that often exists between people. The
code is something like, "I won't challenge you if you won't challenge me." But in breaking that unwritten code, she stepped up
and changed things. I can't be sure how her colleagues reacted.
Knowing the Ritz, they probably appreciated it, but the key is
that she had spoken up, taken responsibility not just for her
guest but for the other guests.

Now I can't guarantee that every time you speak up, the
company will solve a problem and you will become a folk hero. I
can't even guarantee that if you speak up, your career will be better. But I can guarantee you that when people step up by speaking up, real problems often get resolved. I can tell you that years
of research by Dr. Infante and others suggest that stepping up by
speaking up is a great way to raise your profile as long as you are
not just complaining.

What's more, when we don't step up by speaking up, the
consequences can be catastrophic.

The Consequences of Not Speaking Up Can Be Catastrophic

If you want to see the consequence of not stepping up by speaking up, watch the award-winning documentary *Inside Job*,
about the run-up to the financial collapse of 2008–2009 when
the sale of complex derivatives and loose mortgage standards
nearly brought about a Great Depression (and still is having
far-reaching consequences). Surely, lots of people knew that
these practices were dangerous, irresponsible, and at times

unethical. But very few people spoke up loudly and challenged the prevailing paradigm. For some, their failure to speak led directly to the destruction of the very companies they worked for and were supposed to defend.

Think about the Boeing 737 Max disaster, which has cost the airplane manufacturer and the airlines who purchased the airplane hundreds of millions if not billions of dollars. Not only that, but in the case of the Lion Air and Ethiopian Airlines crashes, 346 lives were lost and thousands of friends and family members were impacted. Some engineers and employees did try to speak up to challenge the lack of training for pilots and the making of safety features "optional." But far too few spoke up, and when they did their voices were not heeded. Imagine now the positive benefits that would have accrued and even the lives that would have been saved if more people had courageously simply broken the silence. This is not to say that breaking the silence is easy or without risk, but it is at the very heart of stepping up. It is part of the very essence of being 100 percent responsible.

There is one more very personal reason to speak up. Most all of us have had a time in our lives when a friend or family member spoke up to challenge us in a way that made a positive difference for us. This happened for me recently when I was working on a previous book, a book that had grown out of a personal crisis. After two missed deadlines, a good friend finally spoke up: "I know you have invested a good deal of time into this project but the truth is that you don't want to write this book. It is time to let it go. In this case admitting you made a mistake will open up the space for the book you really want to write."

The next day I called my publisher to pull the plug on the book. It was one of the hardest decisions I have ever made.

STEPPING UP

Three months later I went to Uganda for a month and the idea for this book you are reading was born. If not for the courageous feedback of a friend, I might still be struggling to write a book I did not really want to write.

Speak Up—Your Life Is on the Line

In the end we also speak up because, as one man I interviewed said, your life is on the line. You see, every time we decide not to step up or to speak up a part of us dies.

We have all had the experience of remaining silent and regretting it. When I was a young minister, my second assignment was at an all-white church in Youngstown, Ohio. They were good people, but there was also a strong racist streak among some members. Before the monthly meeting of the elders, a few members often told jokes about black people with offensive phrases like "porch monkeys." As a young minister who had grown up in a family with friends of all races and where people were judged by the content of their character, I found these jokes offensive. The fact that they were spoken before a meeting of elders in a church that professed themselves as followers of Jesus made for a profound (and disturbing) irony.

For months I put up with it in silence. I even laughed nervously from time to time to "fit in." Then one day I finally spoke up. I knew my life was on the line—not my physical life, of course, but my psychic life, my sense of myself as a person. In the middle of one of the jokes I merely said, "You know this is the house of God, not just the house of the white God." The jokes stopped. I offended a few people. A few elders took me aside afterwards and said, "Thank you."

But most of all, I felt good about myself. It may not have changed anyone's mind, but that is rarely the point of speaking up. There were risks as there are always risks in doing the right thing. But truth be told, we may get further ahead by speaking up than by remaining silent, and even if we don't, we will sleep well at night.

Ways to Step Up

✔ **Be constructive.** Starting today, make a commitment to stop being a complainer and to stop being a yes person. Complaining is finger-pointing, not a form of speaking up. Make it your mission to come up with ideas on how things can be better. Be the one who says what others are thinking in a constructive way.

✔ **Challenge your colleagues at work.** Even better, start challenging your friends and family members too. Do what the woman did at the Ritz-Carlton: make it your mission to speak up and make others better, but do it in a respectful way.

✔ **Break the silence.** Enron, the financial disaster of 2008, and many other negative situations might have been avoided if people had been willing to speak up before problems escalated. The world needs courageous people who will challenge the status quo. Doing so may involve breaking the silence about an unethical business practice or challenging a racist comment. Make no mistake, speaking up is a powerful form of stepping up.

CHAPTER 10

Stepping Up or Stepping Back: How to Know the Difference

Your entire life only happens in this moment.
The present moment is life itself.

Eckhart Tolle

Over the last decade, as I have spoken to hundreds of companies and as my colleagues have trained thousands of people on how to step up, one of the most frequent questions that emerged is this: How do I know when I am stepping up? In other words, what are the behaviors that tell me whether I am stepping up or stepping back? Since the choice to step up is made every day in how we act in the moment-to-moment situations of our lives, it is critical for us to understand what behaviors demonstrate stepping up. Once we are aware of what it looks like in practical terms to step up, we can then make a choice to move toward greater responsibility.

Over time we have identified five key behavioral features of stepping up. While these are not meant to be the only five behaviors that represent 100/0 (100 percent responsibility/zero excuses) behavior, together they allow each of us to determine, moment to moment, what it might mean to step up versus step back in most situations both at work and in our personal life.

These behaviors are mapped in a model called the Stepping Up Continuum, which visually depicts what it means to be taking responsibility. The model (fig. 2) has become a tool that organizations can use to communicate the stepping up philosophy while also serving as a powerful visual for each of us to ask: How am I showing up?

Stepping Back 0/100	Stepping Up 100/0
Being Negative/ Pessimistic	Being Positive/ Optimistic
Having a Victim/ External Focus	Having an Initiator Focus
Staying Quiet/ Gutting It Out	Speaking Up/ Seeking Change
Being Closed-Minded/ Defending	Listening/ Learning
Having a Head-Down/ Job Focus	Having a Head-Up/ Impact Focus

Figure 2. **The Stepping Up Continuum**

Being Positive/Optimistic or Being Negative/Pessimistic

The first way we know we are stepping up is if we choose to embrace positivity and optimism, asking what good may be possible in any situation we find ourselves in. Research by Martin Seligman (check out his books *Learned Optimism* and *Flourish*) has shown the many benefits of this mindset, including greater longevity, boosted immune systems, greater physical health, increased happiness, and greater resiliency in the experience of unfortunate events. Being positive is also a strong predictor of leaders' being admired at work, according to studies at the University of Michigan (check out the work of

Kim Cameron and others, including the book *Positive Leadership*). While many of us may quickly grant that optimism is a generally desirable quality, being optimistic is also a key first step in taking responsibility. This same research shows that optimists and those who choose positivity (and yes, this can be learned) react differently to potentially negative life events by focusing on what is possible in a situation.

Let's take an example from the world of work. Pretend your organization is going through a great deal of change that will impact your job in many ways—some worrisome and some potentially beneficial. By choosing to focus on the positive aspects of the change—focusing on what we might gain in terms of new knowledge or even an increased capacity for adaptation in the future—we step toward action. This optimism moves us toward taking full responsibility for what we can do to maximize our learning.

Taking a negative or pessimistic posture, on the other hand, moves us toward passivity. We focus on the change that is being "done to us" instead of the power we have for choosing our reaction to that change. Negativity in any situation can also lead us to a path of chronic complaining, often about external things that we cannot change.

Complaining often is misconstrued as a form of stepping up. After all, we reason, by expressing my dislike of the changes around me, aren't I taking action to generate change? Here I argue the opposite. Complaining and pessimism almost always move us toward passivity. Complaining becomes a substitute for action. Instead of asking what we can do or what we might learn, our complaining becomes a self-perpetuating vortex that keeps us passive. What's more, by chronically focusing on the negative, we will often not take the time to become aware of the possibilities in a situation we may not have chosen to be in.

Since the very essence of stepping up behavior is to focus on the action we can take to change a situation we are in or our reaction to that situation, positivity is required to move us toward acting. Positivity and optimism make us curious about what is possible, while negativity and pessimism often lead to resignation in one form or another. Resignation by its nature is a form of stepping back—of not taking responsibility for what you can do in a situation, however small that action might be.

An extreme example might help demonstrate how optimism leads to action even in the most difficult of human situations. Viktor Frankl was an Austrian psychiatrist and a student of Sigmund Freud who was imprisoned in the Nazi concentration camp at Auschwitz. There is a profound passage in his memoirs where he writes of the moment he realized that the Nazis had taken everything away from him—his possessions, his family, his freedom, and even his dignity. But in that moment, he realized that there was one thing they were powerless to take away from him: his choice of how he would respond to them and to the situation he was in. While it is a great oversimplification, one could argue that in that moment, Frankl chose optimism. Even in the darkest of human experiences, his choice was to look for the positive response, however limited in that situation, which propelled him to action—in this case, the action to wonder what he could still do. Not only did he survive and go on to make a profound global impact through his writing, but he would later advocate persuasively for the role that optimism plays in mental health.

So here, "positivity and optimism" doesn't mean ignoring the hard truth in a given situation but rather recognizing that the moment we focus on what is possible, we are propelled toward whatever action we can take. Earlier in the book we talked about the role naïveté plays in those who step up. The belief that one *can* do something is born in the choice to ask what is possible in any situation. Though action is the prime goal of stepping up, optimism is what propels us to that goal.

Think of the many ways this belief can apply. In an intimate relationship that has deteriorated, positivity about myself and our relationship will turn me toward what might still be possible. A relationship with a difficult colleague will never get better once I harden my mind to the possibility of change because that very pessimism will keep me from choosing action. There is nothing magical about this; it is simply a prerequisite to movement.

I experienced this in my own life when my mother was dying several years ago. The final week of her life in the hospital was both the most difficult and the most rewarding week of my entire life. Since I was an only child growing up in a single parent household, my mother was my rock, and it was incredibly painful to go through the process of letting her go. Yet at the very beginning of that final week, I made a conscious choice to be positive and optimistic. I asked myself this question: What will I learn about myself and about life in this final week? While the week was filled with an ocean of tears, it was also filled with a raging river of lessons. I do believe my choice to be optimistic changed my experience because all that week it forced me to focus on what I was learning, not just on my pain.

Having an Initiator/Action Focus or Having a Victim/External Focus

The second way we can tell if we are stepping up or stepping back in any situation is to check whether we find ourselves focusing on externals we cannot control or on our own power to act. Stepping up means that we focus on what we can do instead of what others need to or can do. It means that we don't waste time focusing on external factors that we are unable to control. If we have the capacity to influence the situation, then we take action to influence it. We recognize that in every situation we are the only part of the equation over which we have control. Hence, when we focus on what we can do, we are inherently in a place of 100 percent responsibility and in a place of empowerment.

While it may sound like a burden to focus on what we can do, it can be incredibly freeing. By focusing on what we can do, we are suddenly freed up to act rather than waiting around for others to do so. Suddenly there is no need to passively wait for something to happen since we become initiators rather than victims.

One of the best ways to know we are in a victim/other focus mode is if we find ourselves thinking or talking about what others need to do. For example, we know we are stepping back when, in an intimate relationship, we find ourselves talking about how our partner needs to change or, in a difficult work relationship, we sit at our desk thinking about what the other person needs to do to make our relationship better. The same is true about a situation in the world or society that bothers us and we find ourselves obsessing and talking about what "they" need to do about this pressing problem.

Now of course, as was said early in the book when we discussed whether our orientation is innie or outie, the world is both. It would be good and useful for others to act—for your partner to change his or her behavior, for your work colleagues to take a hard look at themselves, and for others to take action to solve social problems. But you cannot control them. All you can do is choose to look at yourself and act accordingly.

One of the questions people often ask is, How do I get myself (or someone in my life) into a place of being an initiator rather than a victim? One of the best ways is to ask two simple questions:

- What part am I playing? (What part are you playing?)
- What can I do about it? (What can you do about it?)

These two questions can trigger game-changing shifts. Let's say you think there is not enough romance in your relationship and you want to have more of it. As tempting as it is to make a list of actions your partner ought to take, we know we are stepping up when we ask the two questions above. How am I contributing to the lack of romance in our partnership? What actions could I take to bring more romance into the relationship? The same could be said for that difficult work relationship. We know we are stepping up when we turn the mirror on ourselves to examine our part of the difficulty and identify actions we can take.

The best way to know if you are stepping up is to become aware of the questions that are driving you. Are you asking what others need to do or focusing on what you can do? Are you asking what part others are playing or what part you can play?

The best thing about focusing on what we can do is that suddenly we feel powerful. Also, when we act, it often spurs others to act. Ironically, the best way to get others to step up is to step up ourselves! We cannot control whether anyone else decides to act, but by doing so ourselves we are reclaiming our own power and providing the best opportunity to spur change in others.

We see this even in global affairs. During the now almost two-decade effort to get humanity to cut our carbon emissions, it is not infrequent to hear people say, "What difference does it make if I act but others don't?" I live in Canada and the United States, and people in both countries, even people in places of high influence, say, "Why does it matter if we act unless India and China act?" Though I don't live in either of those other places, it isn't hard to imagine people there saying, "What difference does it make if we act unless the United States does so?" In all cases, the stepping up response is to focus on what *we* can do as opposed to what others need to do. The truth is that because of the responsibility ripple, which was covered earlier, acting like initiators makes it more likely that others will take action.

Focusing on what we can do leans into our power. A personal example is when I first became aware of the impact plastic was having on the oceans and marine systems of the world. As a lifelong conservationist, I was deeply bothered that human garbage was destroying the ocean ecosystem and killing millions of marine birds and mammals. It would have been easier to feel and act like a victim. Yet I knew the stepping up response was to ask the questions I referenced earlier: What part am I playing, and what can I do about it?

Over a period of a year way back in 2007, I moved forward on a series of actions. First, since I live by the ocean and spend a great deal of time near it, I began making it my mission to clean up garbage on beaches that might end up in the ocean. I started posting pictures of the garbage I cleaned up on social media, asking others to do the same. Within a year I had taken a personal pledge to eliminate plastic water bottles, plastic shopping bags, and plastic straws from my life. It took some work, but soon I found that I had reduced my use of single-use plastic to close to zero. I began including plastic pollution in every keynote speech I gave, whether that was the topic of my talk or not. Eventually, much of the world started to catch on to the problem of plastic garbage, though we still have a long way to go to find sustainable solutions. While I can't say what small role I may have helped play in that awakening, I am sure that choosing to focus on what I could do instead of what others need to do provided me with a sense of personal agency.

Rather than sink into a depression, my choice to do what I was able to do gave me a sense of hope.

Speaking Up/Seeking Change or Staying Quiet/Gutting It Out

The third way we can tell, moment to moment, if we are stepping up is to see if we are speaking up or staying quiet. Another way to think of this is that when we are raising issues in a constructive way, we are taking action to move the status quo toward growth as opposed to staying silent or, even worse, moving to a place of passive aggression. The best way to think about the act of speaking up is to inquire as to whether you are asking for what you need in every situation and suggesting ways things could be different. When we stay quiet, we are often choosing not to take the risk of stepping up but to remain passive.

Here are a few examples that help illustrate this point. Let's say there is an issue between me and a work colleague. Let's just say the issue is that I feel my colleague dismisses my opinions and ideas without giving them consideration. Sometimes it even feels to me that this person's behavior borders on rudeness. I feel that my colleague doesn't demonstrate that same behavior toward others. The question is, What does it mean to step up in this situation? Let's apply the first two behaviors. First, I must choose to be optimistic and believe that the situation can change. I must assume that through the right action we can find a place of respect. That optimism propels me toward action instead of passivity. Second, I take time to examine myself. What part might I be playing in the negative tone in the relationship, and what might I do about it? Before even raising the issue with my colleague, I take action to address the ways I may be contributing to it.

Now let's apply the speaking up principle. By staying silent and not being clear on what I see and what I need or want, I am choosing to stay passive. Perhaps I tell other colleagues how I feel but never confront that person directly. Instead of directly speaking up, I make passive-aggressive comments in meetings such as "Well of course you don't like that idea—because it's not yours!" Stepping up means owning what I feel and expressing it in a way that invites others to step up as well.

Speaking up constructively is owning what I feel and the impact on me in a direct way without judgment. Speaking up in this case looks something like saying to that colleague, "I find whenever I give an opinion that I feel dismissed by you because you don't respond to my comments at all or react only in a negative way. The impact is that I feel like you don't respect my opinions and it has negatively affected our relationship. I am quite aware that I may be contributing to the situation as well. I'd like to find a way to improve the situation, and I am wondering how you see it."

Dissecting that response, we see that stepping up is asking for what I need while not judging the other person's intentions and demonstrating my desire to step up to change things. We cannot control how people respond to a genuine request for progress, but we are stepping back when we don't honestly name something, name its impact on us, and ask for what we want.

Of course, as was discussed earlier, stepping up is also about breaking the silence. It is confronting destructive behavior, it is challenging norms or practices at work that could harm the company, it is not remaining silent when we feel there is a better way, and most of all it is finding our voice when we could be silent. Speaking up has been found to be a powerful force in organizational effectiveness.

Listening / Learning or Being Closed-Minded / Defending

A fourth way we know we are stepping up is if we seek and openly receive feedback instead of being closed-minded or defending. One of the most important elements of 100 percent personal responsibility is to take ownership of your own improvement. The opposite of taking ownership is to receive feedback and waste energy defending ourselves against it to protect our ego.

Few things are more valuable to us than feedback, whether it is from a work colleague, an intimate partner, or even a stranger who sees us at work or elsewhere. Yet it is amazing how often our reaction is to be closed-minded and defending. Defending is the stepping back response, while being curious is the stepping up response.

Each of us needs to be aware of how we react when people give us valuable feedback for our improvement. In my experience most people receive feedback something like this: first they say thank you, and then they add a powerful stepping back word, *but*. That reaction is the epitome of stepping back. The *but* response is about going on the defensive. We usually follow the *but* with either an explanation ("Here is why you are not correct with your feedback") or a defense of why we are a certain way or act in a certain way. Our reaction of defense is often not about learning but about protecting the ego. We learn nothing by protecting the ego.

So what is the stepping up response to feedback, whether it is about our work, our style, our communication, or our attitude? If you are a leader, what is the stepping up response when a team member speaks up to provide feedback about you or the organization? The 100/0 response is to be genuinely curious, to wonder what you can learn from this feedback.

When I teach people how to respond to feedback, I suggest a simple technique that has proven powerful. First say thank you in a genuine way. "Thank you for caring about my getting better." Then say, "Tell me more." In other words, instead of defending, get curious. Ask for examples, ask how you might improve, ask for advice, and get genuinely curious about what you might learn.

Often people say, "But what if I don't agree with the feedback?" Well let's say the feedback that people give you is only 10 percent correct (and I think you will agree that is rarely the case). Stepping up and owning even that 10 percent will add a lot more value to your life than defending the 90 percent. By owning the part that we need to improve, we grow our personal reputation and gain valuable insight into how we can do better.

The same is true in a company. When people raise issues, leaders must step up to be curious. We must be in a learning mode rather than a defending mode. We need to do this both because it opens us up to valuable feedback and because it makes it much more likely that people will provide feedback and ideas in the future.

One of the things I have been doing for fifteen years is that after every talk I give, I call the client a week later and ask for specific feedback on how I did, especially for areas of improvement. When I do get constructive feedback, I work hard never to defend but to express genuine curiosity. I admit that sometimes I don't agree with the feedback, and there are times I am very tempted to defend or to explain why I did something. Sometimes I do. But when I do anything besides get curious, I know I am losing the value of learning. I know I am stepping back, not up!

Listening and learning is at the heart of ownership. In an organization, one of our greatest challenges is creating a culture where everyone is listening to customers and col-leagues and leaders are listening to team members. Because I travel often, I always check Travelocity for hotel reviews. One of my pet peeves is the stepping back responses management often posts to seemingly legitimate critiques. On occasion, I see a stepping up response, where management owns what happened and assures the guests that their feedback has been heard. Sadly, this is not the norm. An organization that is truly open to feedback and takes ownership will thrive. Of course, some guests are hard to please and some are mostly wrong in their feedback, but once again we gain more by owning the 10 to 50 percent that is valid than defending our ego.

Stepping up is not just about receiving feedback with an open mind; it is about seeking it on a regular basis. It is about consistently being open to what we might learn from others and what we might learn about ourselves and our organizations by asking. Think about your own life and your own role at work and ask, Do I genuinely seek feedback? Do I genuinely respond with curiosity?

Having a Head-Up/Impact Focus or Having a Head-Down/Job Focus

The final way we know we are stepping up is if we have our head up, trying to see how we can exert influence beyond just our job. *Head up* means we are not just thinking about our immediate impact but thinking about our potential impact beyond whatever prescribed role or job we have. Earlier in the book we saw a few great examples of this, such as the Star-bucks employees in Santa Monica who advocated for an iced coffee dessert drink, which later became the highly success-ful Frappuccino. Developing new products was not in their job description, but they had their heads up, thinking about how they could have an impact far beyond their role. Another example was the story of the two Canadian high school students who stood up to the bullies by getting most of the school to wear pink after a young first-year student was picked on for wearing a pink polo shirt. Once again, no one assigned them that role; they simply had their heads up, looking for how they might have an impact.

This last way of knowing when we are stepping up is most relevant in the world of work, where we often have tightly prescribed roles. When we let our job description limit us, we are stepping back. But when we decide to act beyond our job, focusing instead solely on the question of whether we can have an impact, we are stepping up. One great example of this form of stepping is the story of a frontline supervisor at a large retail liquor company. His organization had a major problem with breakage, whereby product was being broken before it could be sold, costing the organization over $2.5 million a year. Almost all the people involved had their heads down and were blaming others for the problem. The delivery people blamed the stores, the stores said it was the warehouse, and the warehouse team asserted it was the drivers. George worked in the finance department and wasn't responsible for the breakage issue, but he took the initiative by making an appointment with the CEO. At the meeting he said, "Someone needs to solve this problem. I would like you to make it my problem." He told the CEO he didn't want any reward for solving the issue, nor did he even want any time off from his regular duties, he simply asked if the CEO would announce that George was going to lead a group to try to find solutions. It wasn't in his job description, and no one assigned him this role, but he had his head up, he saw a problem outside the scope of his normal sphere of influence, and he stepped up.

Over the next several months he worked hard to get the stores, the delivery personnel, and the warehouse to work together to root out the source of the problem. Within a year breakage had been cut in half, saving the organization over $1 million of recurring revenue. He wound up getting a promotion to be the director of logistics. When the CEO retired eight years later, George was named the new CEO. But it all began when he decided not to be limited by his role and to keep his head up to look at how he could have an influence beyond his assigned place.

Having your head up is about *not* letting your job limit your influence, and it's also about focusing not on your function but on the goal of the larger enterprise. I gave a great example of that earlier in the book when I wrote about the front desk employee at the Ritz-Carlton who was providing me service and observed her colleagues talking to each other while ignoring another guest. Head down behavior would have been to just "do her job," which she was doing well. But in that moment, she had her head up, thinking about not only her success but the success of her colleagues, thinking about the impact she could have on the larger goal of the hotel to win customers and not just her guest—so she spoke up. This is head up, stepping up behavior at its best.

A similar experience happened to me when checking in at an airport. The online check in system wasn't operational, so I had to get my boarding pass at the airport. Having arrived late for a flight I needed to be on, I was told by an agent at the check-in counter that the forty-five-minute check-in window had expired. I begged to be let on the flight to no avail. The agent at the next counter suddenly stepped aside her colleague and said, "Wait a minute. I think I know a way to check you in." Her colleague was not necessarily impressed, but I sure was. She could have simply thought, "Not my customer [which I wasn't], not my problem [which it wasn't]" but she was stepping up to think about the impact for the airline and my loyalty.

Are You in the Red Zone?

One of the ways we move toward stepping up is to consistently ask which part of the continuum are we operating in at any moment—stepping up or stepping back? To our organizational clients we suggest putting the continuum on their desks so moment to moment they can make better choices. Most of us could likely take a few moments to look over that continuum and have a pretty good idea which side we are on. We saw the power of this when, over the course of several years, we designed a program for Qantas Airlines that put almost twenty thousand team members from all levels through a program on stepping up. One of the key metrics of the company's success was its Net Promoter Score, a widely used measure within large companies that assesses customer impressions of the brand. Simply put, the score measures the percentage of customers who say they would highly recommend the company to others and is calculated by subtracting the number of people who provide a score of 0–6 (on a scale of 0–10) from those who score the company 9–10 on their likelihood to recommend it. During that period the company's Net Promoter Scores rose significantly, and the former CEO of the domestic airline division, Lyell Strambi, said, "For the first time when we went through a crisis, it felt like management and employees were on the same page, with everyone focused on their part of the challenge." Though we aren't taking the lion's share of credit for that success, I can say that one of the things that had a big impact was this simple Stepping Up Continuum.

Because Qantas's main corporate color is red, the team members referred to the stepping up side of the continuum as being in the red and the stepping back side as being in the black. "Being in the red" became the code word for being positive, for looking at how you could take action, for speaking up in a constructive way, for listening and learning instead of defending, and for keeping your head up to see how you could take ownership of the customer experience, even if it wasn't in your job description. All one had to say was "Let's get in the red!" The same was true for the other side. Being in the black meant being negative, focusing on what others needed to do instead of taking action yourself, staying quiet or becoming passive-aggressive, tuning out feedback and defending, and focusing only on your function or role rather than the larger goal of providing a great customer experience.

In the end, take the time in each moment to be aware of whether you are in the red or in the black—stepping up or stepping back. You don't necessarily have to refer to these two colors like Qantas did, but whatever code you use, be sure to use it! Of course, we won't always stay in the red. Stepping up is about choosing to be in the red as much as you can be. Even though I teach these ideas every week, I consistently must remind myself, in real moments of action, to move toward stepping up and away from stepping back. If you want to step up more, try to imagine that each day and each moment this continuum sits on the wall and ask yourself, Was I in the red today/in this moment? How could I be more in the red tomorrow/in the next few minutes? You just might find that shift to the right makes all the difference.

Ways to Step Up

✔ **Stay in the red.** Put something red on your desk or in your home in a place that you will see it often. Each time you see it, remind yourself to be "in the red," moving toward stepping up behavior.

✔ **Focus.** Choose one of the five behaviors to focus on for a period of thirty days. Over those thirty days consider that behavior at the start of your day, asking how you might embody it today. At the end of the day, review your day and ask how you embodied that behavior and how you might have done it even more so.

✔ **Get some feedback.** Few of us see ourselves as clearly as others do. While you may have a sense of where you need to focus for change, why not ask for some feedback? Share the five behaviors and the Stepping Up Continuum with a few trusted friends or colleagues. Then ask them where they think you are stepping up and where they think you are stepping back. As you listen to their feedback, make sure not to defend yourself but instead be curious. Practice saying, "Thank you; tell me more."

CHAPTER 11

Creating a Company Culture of Stepping Up

If you treat people like adults, they will act like adults.

Dennis Bakke, former CEO, AES Corporation

Almost all leaders in every company want their people to step up. We want them to act like owners, to have an "it's my job" attitude, and to go beyond whatever their formal role is to take leadership. Parents wish their children would step up and act more responsibly, and teachers want students to step up to the plate. Governments, except those run by autocrats, know the benefit of citizen involvement in solving the great challenges that face them. Having a company, school, or community full of people stepping up can be a game changer. Here are some examples.

Take Harley-Davidson. The company has been making motorcycles since 1912 but by the mid-1980s it was on the brink of bankruptcy. When Harley was almost broke, a group of former executives made an offer and bought the company. In most such crises, companies become more hierarchical. The leaders go off to some hotel, eat shrimp cocktail, make decisions, and come back barking orders. But at Harley, the new owners took a different path. Rather than bark out orders, they asked their people to step up and become leaders. They engaged them in making decisions, asked them to step up and look at their role in making the company successful, and made them a part of the leadership team. They opened up the books and showed everyone what their competitive position was, including that their quality and productivity were considerably lower than their major competitors'. As the company treated people like owners, people started to act like owners. The company's turnaround in profits and market share within four short years continues to make it one of the greatest success stories in modern American business. While the company's star has lost some of its shine because of an aging demographic of Harley customers, its almost two-decade success story following that shift of mindset is legendary.

WestJet is a great success story in Canada and one of the fastest growing airlines in the world. Its whole culture was built on the premise "because owners care." In an industry known for its toxic relationships with employees and its unrelenting punishment of shareholder's wealth, WestJet bucked both trends. It created a place where people at all levels regularly step up and act like leaders while profits grow. WestJet pilots often pitch in to clean airplanes, pack up bags, and do whatever it takes to get a plane in flight on time. It is no accident that the company grew from 0 percent to over 33 percent market share in Canada in just over a decade. WestJet also serves as a cautionary tale about creating an ownership culture. In recent years, insiders say that the culture of ownership has shifted somewhat to a more hierarchical style, which was partially responsible for its pilots choosing to unionize for the first time in 2017.

Schools can also create a culture of stepping up. The success of KIPP in the United States leaves little doubt that things change when you ask people to take responsibility. I asked KIPP's founders how much of the program's success had to do with longer hours in the classroom and how much had to do with character development, that is, getting kids, parents, and teachers to step up. They told me "51 percent is character development," an imprecise guess at what almost every leader knows. By telling students that there are no shortcuts, KIPP teachers let students and parents know that they must first look at themselves and what they can do rather than looking to others to accomplish their goals.

The results of having a company or school (or family) where people act like owners may be evident, but how to create such a place is another story. I have spent a lifetime helping companies and schools create cultures of responsibility, which is why I wanted to ask leaders who had created those kinds of cultures how they did it.

Give People a Seat at the Table

Don Knauss is the former CEO of Clorox, one of the most successful consumer products companies in the world. Don was an officer in the US Marines and did stints in leadership at Coca-Cola, Procter and Gamble, and Frito-Lay before joining Clorox. When I asked him the secret to getting people to step up at work, he had a straightforward response: "People will not step up if you don't give them a seat at the table."

At Frito-Lay, Don was put in charge of a group that delivers and sells chips and snack products in a region in the southern United States. His region was the worst in the country in just about every metric, whether sales per route or amount of product breakage (which basically means the amount of product that can't be used due to damage). Don told me, "The place was filled with tough old drivers who people had given up on years ago. I guess they figured if I could handle Marines, I could handle these guys."

When he took over the region, Don began with two key activities: he told people in the region that he wanted them to go from worst to first, and he gave them a seat at the table. He demonstrated what he called a prevailing optimism, the belief that things could change. Like many others who have stepped up and made things better, he was naïve enough to think he could take this group from worst to first, in spite of the drivers' track record.

"When I took over running that region, one of the first things I did was walk around and talk to the route drivers, one on one, even the old guard who had been there for years and were very entrenched," he said. "I asked them for their ideas on how we could make things better. Of course, I had ideas, but I knew that if they didn't have a seat at the table they would not step up. They shared their ideas and suddenly felt like they were part of things." He started implementing many of their ideas and giving them the credit for it.

Another thing Don did was to force responsibility back on the drivers. He set up a weekly scorecard so that each driver knew how he or she was doing on all the key metrics—sales, breakage, and so on. Then he asked the drivers to meet once every week to go over their scorecards. There was no blaming and shaming, just a chance once a week to compare their performance with others and share ideas for improvement.

Within twelve months the group had achieved Don's vision and gone from worst to first. Later the region won the Herman Lay award for one of the best performing groups in the entire company. Don is humble about his role in that success. "All I did was give people a voice and create a vision that things could be better," he said. "They made it happen."

Years ago, while flying on a business trip, I witnessed the power of giving people a seat at the table. I sat next to a somewhat grumpy middle-aged man. We struck up a conversation and when I told him I wrote books about creating soul in business, he expressed a great deal of skepticism. But when I told him the secret was showing you care about people and giving them a voice, he perked up. He then told me he was the head of the maintenance workers' union for the airline we were on. He said one of the facilities had the lowest quality, worst productivity, and highest number of grievances in the company. The airline replaced the director of the facility with a new leader who spent his first month walking the shop floor to get to know employees as people and to ask for their ideas on how to make things better. Within six months they had the best quality and productivity numbers in the company.

Many leaders are afraid of letting people have a seat at the table because they think frontline people will make the wrong decisions, but this fear is misguided at best. Joanne Beaton's story about taking a dying business at TELUS and turning it into a major profit center was featured earlier in this book. An interesting element of that turnaround is that her first act when she took over operator services was to meet one on one with hundreds of employees. She asked them what they would do if they ran the business and what they would do to put TELUS out of business if they were the competitors. She needed people to step up, to become more productive, and to improve customer service, but she began by inviting them to take responsibility. She gave them a seat.

As part of the research for this book, my publisher and I surveyed four hundred professionals across North America by email to ask them, What do leaders do that keeps people from stepping up? The top answer, selected by 64 percent of respondents, was "leaders making decisions themselves instead of involving others." Although it was not a scientifically selected sample, respondents represented many sectors including both for-profit and nonprofit organizations. We gave them six choices (and also allowed them to write in their own reasons) and asked them to choose their top two selections.

Given the overwhelming desire by employees to have a seat at the table, what exactly do leaders fear that causes them to make decisions without consultation? Joanne Beaton countered the idea that employees will make bad decisions: "Most of the time, given the same information, people will make the same decision as the leader would make. The difference is that when THEY make it, they are much more likely to step up and take responsibility to make the change happen."

Giving people a seat at the table can change the entire culture of a company. In 2008, Darren Entwistle, the CEO at TELUS, formally endorsed a concept called Fair Process across the entire company. Fair Process was designed to ensure that employees were engaged in, and having input into, decisions that affected them. Josh Blair, former TELUS executive vice president for human resources, said this shift has "encouraged employees to step up across the company." Inviting people to have a seat at the table as a formal way of doing business can pay big dividends and may help explain some of the organization's stellar success.

In part, that shift to greater ownership helped TELUS go from midrange employee engagement to best in class in one survey cycle. The survey company communicated that almost all the gains in engagement were in business units where team members had experienced a shift to greater involvement in decisions that impacted them.

A Seat at the Family Table

This same seat-at-the-table principle can be applied in the family. Let's say your teen behaves in a way that concerns you and that calls for some kind of consequences. Imagine if you sat down and gave the teen a seat at the table. Believe it or not, I think in most cases the consequences teens suggest might be aligned with yours or even more severe, but imagine the difference in how they might receive it.

A friend told me that her daughter had posted what my friend considered to be inappropriate pictures on Facebook. The mother could have easily ordered the girl to take the photos down. Instead, she gave her daughter a seat at the table and invited a conversation about what those pictures might say to boys about the daughter. My friend listened deeply, asked good questions, and occasionally led the witness. In the end, her daughter reached the conclusion that the photos were inappropriate. The conversation wound up being a teaching moment, not just a conflict. Her daughter thanked her for engaging in a conversation. The pictures came down by the daughter's choice.

Now don't get me wrong; if it had been my daughter and I felt the pictures were inappropriate, in the end the pictures would come down whether she agreed or not. If the drivers had said, "Hey, let's stay worst," Don Knauss probably would not have gone along with it. The point is, as Joanne Beaton told me, most of the time people (including our kids) will come to the same conclusion we do when we give them a seat.

To Get Responsibility, Give Responsibility

Leaders talk a great deal in the business world about the desire for people to be more accountable. The problem is that we really want people to be more *responsible*. We don't really want to have to watch over people; we want them to voluntarily step up.

One way we create a place where people act more responsibly is to give them more responsibility. That is, if we tie people's hands, they have no reason or need to take personal responsibility. As Dennis Bakke, the former CEO of the AES Corporation, once told me, "If you treat people like adults, they will act like adults. But if you treat them like children, then they will act like children."

Let's take as examples the Ritz-Carlton and the Four Seasons, two of the best customer service hotel chains in the world. At both chains, associates routinely have a large amount of cash at their disposal to create a memorable guest experience and a fair amount of leeway to take action without managerial permission. At the Ritz, associates in even the lower ranking jobs, such as bellhops and housekeepers, have up to a thousand dollars at their discretion to use to create a great experience or thrill a guest. A simple example involved a disabled guest at a Ritz-Carlton resort who was attending a wedding that was to be held at the beach. When staff found out she could not access the beach, they built a platform so she could watch. The platform cost hundreds of dollars to construct, and the managers did not hear about it for days. Clearly, the companies want people to step up and take leadership, and both chains have many stories about people doing just that. But you might wonder how a hotel chain can risk giving people so much discretion.

The answer is quite simple and goes back to Dennis's comment: people who are given responsibility tend to act responsibly. If we want people to step up, we have to have the courage to give them a chance to stumble, to learn, and to grow. They may sometimes go too far, but by giving them power we encourage them to act like leaders.

At WestJet, gate agents and other team members have lots of power to do things right on the spot without asking for permission to please any unhappy customer. Not surprisingly, customers love knowing that frontline people can step up and make things better when there is a problem. But Ferio

Pugliese, the company's former executive vice president of people and culture, told me about a time when a new agent had gone too far, giving out loads of free tickets for a short delay that amounted to a small inconvenience for customers. In some companies she probably would have gotten reprimanded for wasting company dollars. Instead, Ferio said, "We held her up as a good example and then we coached her on how she could do even better next time."

He told me, "The best way to get people to step up is to have spontaneous positive reinforcement for people when they step up and take initiative. The moment you hint that it is not desirable for people to take initiative or step out of their role, then it won't happen again."

It is also amazing how quickly a culture can turn around when we give people more responsibility. Delta Air Lines was once one of the most loved airlines in the world. Filled with southern hospitality, team members had lots of leeway to do the right thing for the customer. Then a series of bean counters became leaders of the company and limited employees' ability to act. Service levels declined and the reputation of the airline suffered.

In recent years, however, service has improved and Delta is often at or near the top of customer rankings. It was even rated in 2018 as one of the most relevant companies in America as defined by positive social media buzz driven mostly by employees. While I have never worked for the company, I have noticed the difference and wondered what happened. Then about six months ago I had to cancel a business trip. I had booked two one-way tickets, so I would incur a two hundred dollar penalty for each ticket. Without any prompting the young call agent said to me, "You know, if you had booked a round trip you would only have to pay one penalty, so I am going to waive the extra penalty." I thanked him and said, "It's great that Delta lets you do that without having to ask for permission." He said, "I have only been here two years, but that is what I love about working here. They let me do what is right for the customer. They empower me to act and I love it."

Getting people to act responsibly by giving them responsibility even works in a family. The sixteen-year-old son of my friend was addicted to high-end clothing, often paying large sums for name-brand sunglasses and T-shirts. His parents got tired of the constant requests for money for clothes, so they decided to give their son the responsibility to manage his own clothes budget. They decided how much they could afford to spend on clothes for him each year and gave him the money in two lump sums in January and July. They said, "Here is your clothes allowance for the year. You can spend it however you want, but if you run out, we won't give you any more money." Suddenly, their son began shopping at discount stores and bringing home five T-shirts for the price he had been paying for one name-brand shirt. Given responsibility, he acted responsibly. Think of all the ways this could be applied in a family, in a school, or within a business enterprise.

Some Surefire Ways to Keep People from Stepping Up

As research for this book, we asked hundreds of people to tell us how leaders keep people from stepping up. They provided a list of surefire ways. As noted earlier in this chapter, the first and surest way is to make decisions without asking for people's input. Sometimes, it is leaders' reactions to people's ideas that matter, which explains why the second most cited (38 percent) thing that leaders do that keeps people from stepping up is "dismissing ideas before exploring them."

Howard Behar was the focus of the Starbucks Frappuccino story I shared earlier in this book. Behar told me the story of a guy who worked for a doughnut chain and sent a memo to his company's president. In the letter he shared a quantity of highly constructive ideas on how to make the restaurants better, how to improve the menu, and how to win loyalty from customers. The man showed Behar the letter he received in response from the company president. Filled with management jargon, the letter basically said, "Thanks for the ideas, they won't work, we have tried them before, you don't have your facts straight, write again soon."

Behar said to me, "Do you think that guy is going to step up and share ideas again?" The guy not only was disappointed but also felt his efforts had been totally ignored. Maybe not all of his ideas were workable, maybe some had been tried before, but the moment the president dismissed his ideas or appeared to not take them seriously, the man, just like most people in similar situations, decided to go back and play the part the company asked him to play. In this case, the man who had written the memo to his CEO as a committed and eager employee now was deflated and soon, perhaps, would join the ranks of cynics.

People do not need many of those experiences before they pull inside their shells like a turtle. Mark Twain once observed that a cat that jumps on a hot stove won't jump on another hot stove any time soon, but it won't jump on any cold stoves either. As leaders, we need to know that every time we discourage someone from stepping up that person is far less likely to step up again. Brigid Pelino, the senior vice president of human resources at Economical, told me that leaders have to be very careful how they respond to people's ideas: "The moment you say 'clear it with so-and-so' or 'we have tried that before,' well, people shut down." She went on to talk about the importance of keeping an open mind. "Don't be so quick to judge, turn off the mouth for a while, and take the ideas in before responding," she advised. I teach leaders a simple method.

Thank You; Tell Me More

Over the years I have discovered some important ways to train leaders to respond more openly to ideas. Let's say someone brings you an idea—for example, a way to have better meetings in the company. Your first response to any ideas should be a hearty thanks: "Thanks for caring about our success." Sadly, the thanks is all too often followed by the dreaded word *but*. "Thanks, but that won't work." "Thanks, but we tried that once." "Thanks, but someone else is working on that." Instead of "thanks, but" try this: "Thanks; tell me more." In other words, get curious and show interest.

Explore the idea, learn what the person has in mind, find out how it might work. If you aren't convinced, you still want to treat everyone like an owner. Instead of saying "That won't work," you can say, "I see merit in your idea but have a few concerns." Once you share those concerns, you can ask, "What are your thoughts?"

Of course not every idea will be a Frappuccino idea, but here is the key point. If you dismiss the not-so-great ideas, there is a good chance that when the Frap idea comes along, people may not even share it. Behar told me the biggest lesson for Starbucks from the Frap experience is that they had inadvertently created a culture that killed ideas. As Linus Pauling, the two-time Nobel prize winner once said in an interview I saw years ago, "The only way to get more good ideas is to tolerate more bad ideas!"

Praise for Effort, Not Just Results

If there is one characteristic that permeates modern corporations, it would be a pervasive focus on results. We judge people mostly by whether they "made the numbers" and achieved the targets we have set. In such an environment, risk mitigation often becomes the norm. Doing what everyone else is doing is a lot less risky than stepping up and innovating. Risk aversion and people stepping up are simply not congruous. The same can be said in a school: the more we focus on results alone, the more we create an environment where students are not eager to step out and take risks for fear of a harsh evaluation. The report card as it is currently used may actually impede growth, rather than stimulate it.

Let's go back to Carol Dweck's fascinating research on mindset. If you recall, she found that children who were praised for effort rather than intelligence were much more likely to take risks on the next task. Perhaps an unrelenting focus on rewarding success rather than highlighting well-thought-out failures and effort creates a climate where people prefer to color inside the lines.

Here is a humorous but telling example. The wife of a friend of mine had been on his case for quite some time about being more romantic. She felt that their relationship had become predictable and boring. After months of her hints, subtle and direct, he checked a book out of the library on ways to be romantic. One Friday night he got home early, prepared a candlelight dinner, and waited, naked, for her arrival. The house was warm, the wine poured, and the dinner ready. When she arrived home, her first words were, "That's not romantic; that is just stupid." He got dressed, they ate dinner in silence, and he took the book back to the library.

Now, he might have chosen a different romantic act as his first attempt, and it may be that his plan would seem more romantic to men than to most women. But when she said that he blew it, she guaranteed that he would not step up again. The organizational equivalent of this scenario happens every day. Someone steps up, plays outside the box, and with one sentence gets shut down.

At the end of the day, it is often fear that keeps people from stepping up. Not surprisingly, 33 percent of our survey respondents said that "creating a climate of fear and compliance" is what leaders do that discourages people from stepping up.

Jim Grossette, the former senior vice president of human resources at Agrium (one of the world's leading fertilizer producers), put it this way: "I've been in places where the moment you do something that does not work, you are going to get slapped on the hand. If people fear for their jobs, or that they will get their hands slapped, or that they will be embarrassed or put down for failure, you will never get people to step up. We need to spend more time catching people doing things right and less time on what's wrong if we want people to step up to the plate."

In my experience, this environment of fear is often very subtle. It can be a frown from a CEO in a meeting; it can be an idea dismissed so quickly that people feel that maybe their job is at risk for even suggesting it; it can be a well-intended risk that went wrong that gets highlighted in a negative light in front of others. If we want people to step up, a certain amount of risk needs to be acceptable. Stepping up and getting it right 100 percent of the time is simply not congruous.

Leaders need to be very intentional about the messages they send to people. For better or worse, an awful lot of people are boss watchers. When I did a tour for senior leaders in the electronic systems division of Northrop Grumman with Jim

Pitts, then the sector president, he told his people, "I hope you are not a boss watcher. I don't want you sitting around waiting to see which way the wind is blowing before you act. If I create an environment of fear, you need to tell me so I can stop doing it." Such messages sent with clarity give people permission to step up, especially when followed up by congruent actions.

Perhaps the keys to getting people to step up at work were best summed up by Ferio Pugliese of WestJet, a company that has spent years building a culture where people are encouraged to take initiative, resulting in stellar business results: "People feel safer in the middle of the herd, but that is not where we want people to be. When you consistently recognize and reward people who disturb the status quo and when people know that you stand for that, then you have a chance of creating something interesting. At the end of the day, people step up because leaders create an environment where it can be done safely."

It's Not about the Horse

Many leaders seem to believe that the way to get people to step up is to handpick their subordinates, almost as if they believe that people's capacity to step up is somehow hardwired. My experience has been quite the opposite. Just about every person I have ever met wants to step up, take initiative, and make a bigger difference. Think about the experience of Joanne Beaton at TELUS. The staff at operator services were not the most likely to step up. The same was true of those drivers at Frito-Lay when Don Knauss took the helm in his area, but great things happen when a leader who truly wants to listen challenges people to step up.

In fact, according to Dennis Bakke, when AES, one of the world's largest power companies, did a worldwide survey of its employees, leaders discovered that employees valued the opportunity to step up and influence their own destiny above almost everything else at work, and that was true in every country the company did business in across Asia, Europe, and the Americas.

If you are in charge and people are not stepping up, it may be best to look in the mirror. Years ago, I had the opportunity to attend a leadership camp that involved helping to train horses. On the first day of the camp our instructor bore a striking similarity in both appearance and demeanor to Curly, the fictional cowboy in the movie *City Slickers*. Within the first hour of our weeklong time with horses, he gave us the most important lesson: "All week long there will be times when the horse will not be doing what you want it to be doing. When that happens, you will be tempted to blame the horse. But I'm telling you right up front that every time you are tempted in that direction, you need to remember that it's not about the horse! Every horse in here is capable and wants to do what we are training them to do. It's not the horse; it's you."

As leaders, as parents, and as teachers we need to remember this lesson. People want to step up, and given the right climate, they will do so.

Societal Implications

Countries and communities also have a stake in creating a place where people will step up and take responsibility. Whether in small matters like keeping a neighborhood safe or in large matters like solving climate change, we need individual citizens to take action. There are simply not enough police to keep us safe, just as there are not enough sanitation workers to keep the oceans free from garbage. There is little doubt that the financial crisis of 2008 was manufactured in boardrooms and government agencies, but anyone who bought a house without understanding the potential impact of higher interest rates or a slump in prices was equally culpable. Only when we begin to see that individual responsibility is at the heart of a healthy society will we begin to make real progress toward solving the great challenges of our day. Even as I write this the world is in a panic over the COVID-19 coronavirus. A medical professional was being asked during an interview what the government needed to do. After he finished he said, "But every individual will have as big an impact on this situation by washing their hands, keeping their distance, not touching surfaces, and so on."

This idea came home to me in a very personal way in my city of Vancouver in June 2011. The Vancouver Canucks hockey team was playing in the seventh game of the Stanley Cup finals against the Boston Bruins. Over 150,000 people gathered to watch the game on large television screens in the downtown core while the teams played at the arena six blocks away. Hockey is serious business in Canada, and Canucks fans had waited almost twenty years for a shot at the championship. Just a year before the city had proudly hosted the 2010 Winter Olympics and had been praised worldwide as a gracious host.

The Stanley Cup game did not go well, and the Canucks took a crushing defeat in their quest to win their first championship. Downtown, alcohol and stupidity combined to escalate fan unhappiness into a series of riots. Crowds overturned and burned police cars, broke store windows, and looted merchandise. The outnumbered police did their very best, but Vancouverites watched their televisions in horror as all that good will from the Olympics went up in the dark smoke that I could see from my balcony.

As I watched the live news coverage, I kept wondering, *Why are so many citizens standing around taking pictures of the riots and looting?* Why aren't people stepping up to take action? Often, there appeared to be only a few troublemakers surrounded by hundreds of bystanders. It was not until the next day that stories started to emerge of citizens who had stepped up. A young woman stood by a car that was about to be burned as a crowd taunted her, but she stood her ground. It was not her car.

A shopkeeper watched in dismay on television as stores were looted on his street of business, certain that his store, too, had been badly damaged. Around midnight he got a call from a stranger telling him that his store was undamaged. He asked the man on the phone how he knew this to be the case. The stranger said he knew because he and several other citizens had stood watch by the storefront, keeping looters away. They were not friends of the store owner, and only one of those responsible had ever even been in the store.

The next morning hundreds of local residents showed up downtown in the early morning hours with brooms and supplies to clean up the mess. No one had asked them to come. One mother arrived with her young daughter, both with hands in rubber gloves ready to get to work. When she was interviewed she said, "I just wanted my daughter to know this is what people do."

To be honest, some good Samaritans did not fare so well the night of the riots. A few got beaten up, and many were taunted. Yet one cannot help but wonder how the night might have been different if hundreds instead of scores had stood together to defend their city's image. If those who had taken pictures had decided to be active instead of observers, might the night have had a different ending?

The point is that many did step up. They did not see it merely as the job of police or of city workers. They saw a problem and decided they were the ones who could do something about it. Leaders in government must have the courage to challenge people to step up and at the same time give them a seat at the table. Only when we are asked to be responsible will we likely act responsibly.

Ways to Step Up

✔ **Build a "seat at the table" leadership style.** One of
the best ways to nurture this style is to make daily
"rounds." This term comes from health care, where
doctors make visits daily to each patient. Leaders
should make daily rounds by walking around and
checking in with team members to find out what is
happening in their lives, ask them for ideas to make
work better, and express appreciation for work well
done. Some research suggests that making daily
rounds increases customer and employee satisfaction
up to 25 percent! Other ways to nurture this style
include having monthly "make it better" meetings,
inviting groups of staff members to have an informal
breakfast or lunch with you on a rotating basis, having
town halls, and generally making it clear you want
people to express their ideas (even if they disagree
with yours). Remember, the more we give people a
seat, the more they will take it.

✔ **Watch your reaction, *always*.** Remember, as formal
leaders, we are always on stage when it comes to
encouraging people to step up. Even a hint that we
want people to "stay between the lines" will shut
down innovation. Remember the two ways survey
respondents said we keep people from stepping
up—not asking for their opinion and dismissing ideas
without exploring them.

✔ **Praise effort.** Go overboard to praise effort as well
as results, especially if people go beyond their role
and really step up.

CHAPTER 12

Who Am I to Step Up?

There are no extraordinary people, only ordinary people who do extraordinary things.

Mother Teresa

When people think about stepping up and creating change, they often ask, "Who am I to step up?" Of course I could easily turn that around and ask, "Who are you *not* to step up?" As I interviewed people who had stepped up, I increasingly was struck by the fact that stepping up is not about being extraordinary. In fact, I found that often those who stepped up were unlikely candidates.

Homeless to Hero

Ken Lyotier is a case in point. By his own admission, at the time he began a recycling revolution and later created jobs for hundreds of homeless people, he himself was an alcoholic Dumpster diver in Vancouver making his living by salvaging discarded bottles. Just how he got to that state of affairs and how he stepped up to create change is the stuff of urban legend.

Ken was raised just outside of Vancouver and had a pretty normal upbringing in a working class family during the 1950s and 1960s. When he was seventeen years old, he went to study at the University of British Columbia. At the same time he began to take ill. By the time he was diagnosed with severe Crohn's disease, a form of inflammatory bowel disease, the illness had wreaked havoc with his health, his social life, and his studies. He never finished his degree.

"They didn't know what was wrong with me, and it took a very long time to diagnose it," he said. "For a decade I was sick, diarrhea all the time. It was very isolating. I simply could not commute to school any longer, so eventually I had to drop out. I sold real estate for a while, was involved in land title, basically had a good life but also discovered alcohol and drugs. It is a long story, but I wound up homeless and a Dumpster diver. I lost my job and eventually the money ran out. For some time I was homeless."

He was not exactly on the most-likely-to-step-up list. His description of life as a homeless person is riveting and heart-breaking. He told me stories of the daily indignities homeless people had to face to scrape together a meager existence. I also learned that the stories of how people fall on such hard times are very human and unique to each person.

Yet his life rummaging in garbage bins gave him a unique vantage point both on the amount of waste that people create as well as on the indignity that the indigent people face daily. Ken told me this story: "At the time there were very few prod-ucts in the recycling deposit system—Pepsi, Coke, and a few beer companies. So to make a living you had to really work hard to find enough to live. Even worse there was the indignity of it all. Stores had a limit on how many bottles you could bring in at one time, and they did not like having these dirty, smelly street people in their stores. People were treated so poorly and often manipulated. For example, store owners would make the homeless buy something from the store in order to give the deposit money. A lot of people who live a normal life have no idea how hard many homeless people work to get a few dol-lars. This image of a lazy bum is far from reality."

In 1991 while still diving Dumpsters for a living, Ken and another homeless man, Williams Tremblay, had a chance conversation in a coffee shop with a United Church of Canada minister about the problems and daily challenges the homeless binners faced. The United minister said he had access to a little bit of money if Ken had an idea on how to make things better. Although that minister would not be central to the story that evolved, his willingness to put forward $1,500 to a pair of street people was an act of great faith.

Ken came up with an idea. "As binners, we had a close-up view of people's garbage, and I was amazed at how much was being thrown out—tons of bottles and cans that could not be recycled. So we had this idea of a one-day event where people would be invited to bring any nonrecyclable bottles they could find to a particular place on a Sunday morning, and they would get paid for the bottles that were not in the deposit system." Ken hoped it would raise awareness about both the plight of the so-called Dumpster divers as well as the sheer amount of waste people were creating. They advertised the event by posting fliers on Dumpsters, offering ten cents for small bottles and twenty-five cents for the big ones. Ken had no idea how many people would show up.

When the day came, Victory Square in Vancouver had a line that wrapped several times around the block. Hundreds of homeless people showed up, and by the end of the day there was a huge mountain of garbage. Of course most of the street people came for the prospect of earning ten dollars, but Ken was overwhelmed.

"People were lined up, and I thought, 'We did this!' It was so energizing and profound, like the loaves and fishes in the Bible, they just kept coming. It made us want to do more. I thought, 'Wow, if we can do this, then I wonder what else we can do?'"

The mountain of garbage and the march caught the media's attention. The idea that two binners had organized such an event captured the imagination of the public and the government. As a result of publicity from the event, the provincial government promised to bring scores more products into the recycling program. Even though it took years to fulfill that promise, Ken and Williams helped spawn a recycling revolution. These two Dumpster divers helped set in motion a chain of events that led to scores of additional products being recycled over the next twenty years. The mountain of garbage they helped prevent is almost unfathomable.

Ken told me, "It was a kind of protest that day against what was being thrown out and the indignities faced by the homeless, but most protests are people with signs marching against something. Instead, we did a good thing and just said, 'Come and look at how things could be.'"

If the story ended there it would be inspiring, but Ken's story of stepping up was far from over.

If anger is one thing that spurs us to step up, then seeing how powerful we are is another major stimulant. When Ken saw what could be accomplished by posting those fliers on the Dumpsters, it made him want to do more to make a difference. That compounding effect is why it is important to take that first action: once we see how powerful we really are, it becomes much harder to stay on the sidelines. As the Coldplay lyric says, "If you never try you'll never know / just what you're worth."

Emboldened by the experience from Victory Square, Ken became an advocate for his fellow Dumpster divers. When the government started hiring consultants to research the implementation of the new recycling deposit system, Ken pushed for a series of town hall–type sessions to get input from the homeless and binner community. He told the government that the homeless people were consultants just as much as the high-priced advisers the government had hired, and he cajoled the government to pay ten dollars to each person who attended the meetings.

Partly as a result of those town hall meetings, Ken hatched a larger idea. He recalled, "People came to those meetings, and I remember one woman who had all kinds of problems and addictions talking about how she was treated at the stores, how they made her buy gum with the money or they would not give it to her. She told us, 'I have no dignity.' So I had this idea to create a bottle depot of our own, a depot where the homeless could come and be treated with dignity."

More than that, Ken envisioned a place where all the employees would be Dumpster divers. When he first started talking to people about his idea, people thought he was nuts. "The idea kept bubbling along for a few years," he said. "Honestly, I was still making a living with bottles so I had to do this in my spare time." But Ken kept pushing until finally a window of opportunity opened when the city was building a new sports arena and made a commitment to employ poor people from the downtown eastside into the workforce. Ken told the government that his bottle depot could serve as a test lab for training street people to enter the workforce. His years of hard work and persistence finally paid off, and the bottle depot was born.

"It was hard. We became a nonprofit and even had a board, but I was still fronting the money for the pizza. The idea of the homeless working at the arena never came to pass, but the depot opened. Early on, I needed to get a line of credit, and I didn't even know what one was at the time. Imagine the banker's face when I came in asking for one!"

Today, United We Can continues to run a bottle depot and an urban farm called Sole Foods in Vancouver, right in the heart of one of the poorest neighborhoods in the developed world. United We Can eventually came to recycle millions of products a year, turn a profit, employ scores of homeless people, and contribute to a recycling revolution. Ken is retired and on the organization's board, and, with the exception of the executive director and the manager of the urban farm, the staff is made up entirely of binners, some homeless, who have found a place of dignity through work. Some gave up their addictions, some did not, but all found something at the depot. Every day hundreds of homeless people bring their bottles and cans to the depot and are treated with respect. The homeless Dumpster diver had become an entrepreneur and an activist. He had raised awareness in the Victory Square rally and persevered until he created a thriving enterprise.

When I asked him to tell me a few stories about the difference the depot has made in people's lives, he told me about the first Christmas after it opened.

"We had been open for about a year, and we had a party for the staff and whoever wanted to come," he said. "People came to that thing, and we sat around and drank and talked. These folks had no place to have Christmas. They came, and it was not a bar, not the street or a hotel room. There was this sense of community. I remember the laughter, people talking to each other about memories of their Christmases past. They so needed that. It gave me a lot of comfort and hope, seeing people so alive and engaged. To be reassured that they somehow knew there was hope, that no matter how miserable their lives can be they can still find a place to connect."

And then there were the stories of those individuals whose lives changed.

"There was a guy who had been fostered out and adopted many times as a child," Ken said. "He had drifted from place to place and finally was working with us at the depot. He had taken on some supervisory responsibilities, but there was a street altercation and he was beaten up badly. He told me, 'That's it. I'm gone.' He just wanted to move on, the way he had probably done all his life. I said, 'You have some vacation time—take it.' I let him know he was valuable and there was a place for him here. 'We are not letting go of you even if you leave.' Later on, he said to me, 'I don't want to move on, I am tired of moving on.' That guy stepped up more and more and eventually became a very valuable person taking on lots of responsibility. In time he got his own apartment and settled down."

For every victory there have been defeats, but Ken has no doubt that the depot has changed lives.

Skill Is Not as Important as Passion

Ken's story reminds us that position or even skill, per se, are not the prime attributes of those who create change. To step up does not require being extraordinary or having extraordinary means. It is about having the heart, the perseverance, and the desire to make something happen. It is about having a vision. Once you step up, somehow that act of taking initiative drives you to find the resources you need inside and outside yourself. If Ken had worried about whether he was the right guy or whether the resources would be there, he never would have accomplished so much. Instead, he had a vision, and the resources somehow materialized.

Perhaps what people responded to in Ken was more important than intelligence or resume. Study after study shows that the one quality all great teachers have is passion. We are attracted to passion and to vision. Think of the stories of those who have stepped up that have been told in this book. All of those who made something happen had two things in common, passion and determination. These qualities are infectious and make others want to help us.

It may be that almost every person who has ever stepped up doubted that she had the resources, talent, and skill to do so. You may doubt that you are the right person to step up. Yet what I learned in this research is that skill, talent, and resources are overrated compared with drive, determination, and vision.

Helping Women Out of Poverty, One Bead at a Time

Devin Hibbard is the CEO and cofounder of an organization called BeadforLife. Over the last sixteen years, the organization has helped over ninety thousand women in Uganda escape the cycle of extreme poverty by starting their own businesses. BeadforLife began because of a chance meeting in 2004 that Devin Hibbard and her BeadforLife cofounders, Torkin Wakefield and Ginny Jordan, had on a visit to a refugee camp in Kampala, Uganda. The camp was filled with women, many of whom were HIV-positive or AIDS widows who had fled a civil war in northern Uganda. A woman named Mille showed the three the jewelry she had made out of beads created from recycled paper. She told them that she worked all day crushing rocks at a quarry for one dollar per day. Her beads were beautiful, but she said she had no market to sell her work. Devin and the others bought some of Mille's jewelry, not realizing that their lives and the lives of thousands of women were about to change.

When they came home, the three women showed the beads to friends and told the story of the Ugandan women's lives. In September 2004 they invited friends to a bead party, and the guests loved the jewelry. An idea began to hatch in the women's minds: maybe they were being called to create a market for these Ugandan women's work.

"The funny thing is that at New Year's we had set some intentions together for the year, and one of those intentions was to do something for the world," Hibbard told me as we sat in her humble office in Kampala, Uganda's capital city. Hibbard is a deceptively powerful and magnetically attractive woman who runs a tight ship but is deeply loved by her Ugandan staff. When I met her for the first time, she had just returned from a month in the United States, and the offices were filled with notes and pictures about how much she had been missed. Her style is matter of fact, but her passion for this mission and for life is contagious.

"Frankly, we did not have a grand plan, or any real credentials to do this," she told me. "We had no marketing experience, no retail experience, and no grand plan, but we felt like the universe was knocking at our door and figured if the universe was knocking who were we to say no! We just kind of leapt into the unknown and took it step by step."

Within a few years, bead parties were happening all over the United States. In Uganda, BeadforLife took in groups of women who were in desperate poverty and trained them to make the beads and jewelry. The organization stabilized the women's lives with a steady income from the beads, trained them to start more traditional businesses, and gave them a grant if they had a solid business plan. Eventually, BeadforLife bought a large piece of land outside the city and created a community called Friendship Village where women and families could buy modest new homes with the beads they supplied to BeadforLife.

When I visited Uganda for a month in August 2010, I visited the homes and businesses of many women who had been through the BeadforLife program. Again and again

I heard stories about how making these beads had changed these women's lives. What I learned is that BeadforLife was not just eradicating physical poverty but also poverty of the spirit. BeadforLife had helped women believe in themselves and in the possibility of dreaming again.

One young woman named Fiona is in her late twenties. She was an AIDS widow at a very young age, destitute and with children. Other women in her neighborhood nicknamed her Old Young because she looked so very old for being so very young. "When I passed the cemetery," she said, "I envied the dead." Then she told my companions and me what happened when she met the people from BeadforLife: "They taught me how to make beads and jewelry but more importantly they taught me to believe in myself." Today, Fiona lives with her two children in a home she owns in Kampala, and stores in Seattle and Vancouver sell her jewelry. She is independent of BeadforLife, leaving room for other women to join the program.

Today, Devin leads an organization with more than sixty staff members and interns, almost all Ugandans in Kampala. Every year, several hundred more women and families are lifted out of poverty, all because three women with few credentials but lots of heart decided to step up. Devin gave me a great definition of stepping up: "Stepping up is seeing a need and deciding you are the right person to do something about it!"

"You have to step out of your comfort zone. I mean, we had very little experience for doing what we did, but the resources came to us once we stepped up," she told me. When I asked Devin about advice for others, she gave me some important counsel. "To step up you need patience. We are so wedded to instant gratification, but if you want to change things you have to know it won't happen right away."

It is an important lesson. It took years before Rex Weyler's picture led to the banning of the whale hunt. Ken Lyotier stepped up and the government promised to recycle more, but it took years of persistence to make good on that promise and begin the bottle depot. BeadforLife is a thriving organization that is making a huge difference in Uganda and is part of a much larger movement to empower people in the developing world. BeadforLife has an inspiring and simple mission statement: BeadforLife creates sustainable opportunities for women to lift their families out of extreme poverty by connecting people worldwide in a circle of exchange that benefits everyone. To learn more about its work or to host a party, go to www.beadforlife.org.

The Two Voices

What I learned is that many of those who stepped up had this thought: who am I to do this? Devin Hibbard started BeadforLife with no marketing or retail experience but a great desire to get something done. Joanne Beaton had never run operator services but wanted to create a thriving business. Rahul Singh was a paramedic, not a fundraiser. Ken Lyotier was diving in Dumpsters but stepped up anyway. The Starbucks manager in Santa Monica was not a marketing guru, but she knew a good thing when she saw it. Mike Feinberg and Dave Levin were brand new teachers, not entrepreneurs, but started an alternative public school system. David Shepherd and Travis Price were just normal twelfth graders when they began a pink shirt revolution.

So maybe the question really is: who are you not to step up? Whatever reasons you have to say you are not the right person, you can be sure that someone else had those same thoughts and stepped up to get something done. Mike Feinberg, one of KIPP's cofounders, put this in perspective: "There is often a voice inside of us that says I am not good enough or qualified enough to do this, but there is another voice that says we can do it. Too often we give that negative voice too much power."

Ken Lyotier knows that negative voice all too well, but he also heard another voice. His parents died while he was living on the streets. Some years after his mother's death, he was diving in a Dumpster one day in Stanley Park in Vancouver when he came upon an urn used for human ashes. "Someone had probably put the ashes in the water at the beach and then thrown the urn away. As I handled the urn I could hear my mother's voice saying, 'Ken, there must be something more you can do with your life than dive in Dumpsters.'"

A few weeks after I met Ken, he learned that he would be receiving an honorary doctorate—a distinction given to very few—from the University of British Columbia, the school he had dropped out of because of illness forty years earlier. Life had come full circle. With tears in his eyes he said, "I just wish my parents could be alive to see this."

Ways to Step Up

✔ **Remember what matters.** Whenever you are tempted to step up and think you don't have the talent, skill, or qualifications, remember that vision, determination, and perseverance are the most important qualities of those who step up. When that voice says, "Why me?" replace it with, "Why not me?"

✔ **Do something!** Take a step you don't think you are qualified to take to try to change something.

✔ **Embolden others.** Always encourage someone who says they want to step up, even if you think they are not qualified. Your word of encouragement could make a big difference. Remember the United Church minister is the one who encouraged those two homeless men to take a step. Imagine if he had not done so.

CHAPTER 13

One Person *Always* Matters

> It is from numberless diverse acts of courage and
> belief that human history is shaped. Each time
> a man stands up for an ideal, or acts to improve
> the lot of others, or strikes out against injustice,
> he sends forth a tiny ripple of hope.
>
> Robert Kennedy

Much of this book has danced between two concepts, the need
to take responsibility and the results of what happens when we
step up to take action. I hope that by now you are convinced
that looking in the mirror is better than pointing blame; that
when we focus on what we can change rather than what others
need to change, we move into a place of power; that even if only
a small portion of any problem is ours, something important
shifts when we decide to take 100 percent responsibility for
that part; and that taking responsibility creates a ripple that
spreads. This final chapter focuses on the second concept, that
one person stepping up really matters.

Most of us have at least one time in our lives when we
know it mattered that we stepped up, that something was different because we chose to act. Just before I sat down to write
this chapter, I went to cast my vote in a local election, and on
my way back I picked up several plastic bottles off the sidewalk
to throw into the recycling bin. I might rightfully wonder if it

really mattered that I decided to take those two actions. They are both acts of faith.

When I think about my own experiences, I can think of several times when I do believe my stepping up mattered. I grew up on Staten Island, one of the five boroughs of New York City. At the time the island still had lots of green space, even farms. As the population grew, green space turned into burgeoning housing developments and roads. Rows and rows of cookie-cutter housing developments replaced the island's parklike beauty. In the middle of the island, however, there remained a circle of green—a series of parks and natural areas that remained intact—that came to be called the greenbelt.

When I was in high school, a major fight erupted over the future of the greenbelt as new development threatened to break the circle of green. Over the preceding years, many people had helped to preserve the belt, and now decisions would be made that would forever determine its fate. Along with many others, I stepped up to express my views, helped write articles about the greenbelt, and even participated in protests. I have not lived there for almost fifty years, but flying over Staten Island on a recent business trip I could see that beautiful ring of uninterrupted green right in the center of the island. Thousands of people had stepped up, and there is little doubt that if we had not done so, that green would have long melted into the urban sprawl that enveloped the smallest borough. It is a small victory in the larger scheme of things, perhaps, and not one I can claim as mine alone, but I am sure that if people (including me) had not stepped up, things would have been different.

The many stories in this book bear ample witness to the power of stepping up. Joanne Beaton and her team at TELUS saved the operator services business; the woman on the bus saved the life of a stranger contemplating suicide; Devin

Hibbard's choice to start BeadforLife changed the lives of thousands of women in Uganda; children went to University and graduated who would not have done so because Mike Feinberg and Dave Levin chose to create an alternative school system; Starbucks continued to reward shareholders handsomely partly because one store manager in Santa Monica kept on pushing; homeless people found new dignity because of Ken Lyotier; whales swim still in the wide oceans in part because of Rex Weyler; and a Canadian Tire collection agent changed the life of one customer while helping to create customers for life.

But there is more. In each of these cases, the starring cast is much larger than it appears. Think of the people who hold BeadforLife parties every year across Europe and North America, doing their own stepping up. The money they have raised is as much a part of helping women out of poverty as what Devin Hibbard does in Uganda. Think of all those who wrote letters to save the whales, signed petitions, made phone calls to politicians, walked in marches, and so on. They are the real reason whales roam free. Sure, that agent made one customer for life, but the future of a company and its reputation are in the hands of thousands of employees who will make a choice this very day to step up and be counted.

One person always matters, and one person acting in concert with others—what I referred to previously as aggregate influence—matters even more. In fact, my advice to you is always to assume that others are acting. When we assume others will act, we often decide to claim our power. In fact, research shows that if you tell people to vote because turnout is low, voting is actually suppressed. Apparently, people think something like, "Since no one else is voting, why should I vote?" On the other hand, that same research shows people who hear a message such as "a record number of people will vote" are much more likely to act, presumably because they feel both that it matters but also that they might be left behind by not voting. The same has been found to be true in hotels that are trying to reduce use of towels and change of bed sheets for environmental reasons. Simply by putting a note in the bathroom that says "Eighty percent of the people who stay in this room choose not to have their towels changed every day" significantly increases the number of people who make that choice. In other words, the perception that others are stepping up actually causes others to step up. This is why what we do matters so very much. And that's why I think we should always assume others are taking action. The worst that can happen is we are wrong and will have acted nobly anyway.

Step Up ... or Live to Regret It

One of the most important reasons to step up is that most of the time we regret *not* stepping up. As Rahul Singh told me, "Life is short, and you don't want to wonder what might have happened if you had stepped up." It was this very realization following his best friend's death that compelled Rahul to start Global Medic even though he had no experience raising funds or running a nonprofit.

Life gives us many opportunities, and those opportunities require us in one form or another to raise our hands and say, "Count me in." As one person told me, "There are always voices telling us not to step up, a voice telling us that we are not good enough, skilled enough, worthy enough." But these voices are not our friends.

In 1994 I had the privilege of attending the UN Conference on Population and Development in Cairo, Egypt. Although I went there representing an environmental organization, I was only a volunteer and not an employee of that organization. As part of a conference run alongside the UN conference by

NGOs (non-governmental organizations), I had no particular authority. The job of the NGOs was both to influence the official delegations that had gathered to tackle the daunting human challenges of sustainability and to help win the media war, to tell the story of why it mattered so much that we act.

The first day of the conference, all the environmental organizations from around the world gathered together, meeting by region. I found myself in the North American caucus surrounded by scores of qualified people, most of whom were full-time environmental activists. Organizers told us that each region needed to select a chairperson to represent the caucus. As we gathered together, I thought about putting my hand up, but then I thought, "Who am I to be the chair, since many of these folks are full timers with a lot more experience than I have?" Still, I wanted to have influence; I wanted to step up. In that moment I thought of other times in my life when the chance had come to step up and I had not done so out of fear of failure. Suddenly, my hand was in the air. "I will do it," I blurted. Before anyone had the opportunity to suggest an alternative, someone had seconded the motion, and the chair was mine. You could see the stunned faces of the more qualified candidates who probably had expected to be selected but had held back for whatever reason.

For the next two weeks I had the time of my life. I attended daily meetings with Timothy Wirth, the head of the US delegation, and got to have my say directly about what our caucus felt needed to happen. Numerous media outlets interviewed me, and one interview ran on National Public Radio's *Morning Edition* all across America. One of my clients called to say she was in the shower when she heard me on NPR and almost slipped and fell! I also learned a great deal about issues that mattered to me and felt that the experience led to other choices to step up later.

As the conference wound down, several members of the North American caucus confided in me that they had wanted to volunteer to be the chair, but they had hesitated in part because they had listened to that other voice we have talked about. Having seen how much fun I had and how much influence I wound up having, they told me they were sorry that they had not raised their hands.

What might you step up to do right now in your life if you knew you might regret not doing so later on? It might be stepping up at work to say what others are thinking but will not voice. It might be volunteering to write an article or lead a project or simply to change how you are acting in relationships. One thing is for sure, as United We Can founder Ken Lyotier reminded me, "It is safer to stay on the sofa and watch the game, but you will never know what you are capable of until you step up." He stepped up, and in spite of years of homelessness and alcoholism, he wound up influencing thousands of people's lives, earning an honorary doctorate, and helping to spawn a recycling revolution. He might not have felt good enough to put his hand up and say "pick me" and might even have doubted his own voice, but step up he did.

This is the time to step up, *right now*. It may not matter if you do so, but you won't ever know if you don't.

The world is always different when we step up. Something changes in the field of energy when people take initiative. Your voice may be one of many or wind up putting you at center stage. But those who wrote letters to save the whales were as important as those who ran after the Russians in rubber Zodiacs, and those operator services staff members who changed their behavior were as important as the woman who led them.

What I Learned from a Pile of Rocks

All of us wonder if what we do really matters. As you recall when we asked those hundreds of people in a survey why they don't step up more, the largest response by far was "I can't change things/I am only one person." It has often occurred to me that one of the greatest challenges of our day is the feeling of impotence—but not the kind that can be fixed with a little blue pill. This is the impotence that comes from feeling like we are powerless to wield influence whether at work, in society, or even in our personal lives as witnessed by a several-decade shift toward an eternal locus of control on Rotter's scale, referenced earlier.

This question loomed over me in the summer of 2019 as I walked the Camino de Santiago for the second time. This 750-kilometer walk across the north of Spain began twelve hundred years ago as a pilgrimage for Christians but is now routinely taken by people of many faiths, nationalities, and ages. The one common denominator in my experience is that almost everyone who chooses to take the thirty-day walk is on some kind of personal quest.

Near the height of the walk is the Cruz de Ferro, which is about 222 kilometers from the end of the traditional path at the cathedral in Santiago. The iron cross sits atop a mound that has developed over the centuries where pilgrims by tradition leave a rock or stone to symbolize their journey. It is a place of great emotion for people who take this path.

The first time I arrived at this place, when I walked the camino for the first time in 2015, I found myself overwhelmed with emotion. Here was a place where for over one thousand years, an untold number of people from all over the world have left a rock to symbolize their life's journey. It occurred to me that there were two possible reactions to this giant pile of human-placed rocks.

One response is to be stricken with a sense of how unimportant your rock truly is. After all, the vast majority of the people who have laid these rocks are long gone and most remembered now by no one. Some painted their rock or left a note attached to it to make their rock stand out, but these rocks sit now with colors long ago faded and notes blown away or withered by time. "What," I thought, "does it matter if I place one more rock on this pile?"

But there is a another, wholly different response one can have approaching that hill, and this was what welled up in me. In that moment I realized that I was a part of a very large and long conversation, one that had begun thousands of years before my arrival and may well go on for thousands after I placed my rock. While my one rock might seem insignificant, it was a part of the entire human journey of which I am a full participant. This hill was representative of something much bigger than myself. My rock was significant *precisely* because it was part of a large conversation. All human progress, all good things accomplished from the abolition of slavery, the rights of women, the emergence of democratic ideals, and even the success of a particular organization were all built on the foundation of a rock that was laid before mine.

Stepping up is about choosing to put your rock on the pile of human progress or even the progress of your small part of humanity—your family, your team, your organization. Your rock matters. Everything that has ever been accomplished has happened because people like us put our rock down. Each of us is the descendant of a long list of survivors who placed a rock in hopes of a better future for the next person who would place one. Placing our rock, stepping up, is ultimately an act of faith—one I hope you will take.

So … You Have a Choice

Ending a book is always a great challenge. On the one hand is the desire to end with something profound, some memorable words to send you out. Yet again and again I am reminded that the end of a book is never written by an author; it is written by the readers. One of the most rewarding things about being a writer is that often, out of the blue, people will send me an email, write a letter, or call me to tell me how something in one of my books lit a fire in them, changed their perspective, spurred them into action, or merely gave them comfort in an important period of their life. Just a few weeks ago, a man told me that he and his wife keep a copy of my book *The Five Secrets You Must Discover Before You Die* on their bedside stand. He told me that they often read a passage right before bedtime. He went on to tell me that they had recently made a decision, spurred on by my book, to take six months off to visit family overseas and give the grandchildren a chance to spend time with grandparents before it was too late. They had sacrificed some money, but the sacrifice had been worth it.

I cannot be certain what you might do because you read this book, but it is my fervent hope that you will do something. It is my hope you will focus even more on taking responsibility and even less on pointing fingers. I hope you will stop trying to get others to change and focus even more on trying to change yourself. I also hope that you will assume you can change things and do what you can, while encouraging others to step up even if it seems naïve of them to try. Maybe some of you will be the next Devin or Rahul or Ken or Joanne. Maybe you will simply step up more actively and make a bigger difference in your five rows of influence. The world is waiting for you. It is waiting for each of us. One person stepping up always matters. It is all that matters.

So repeat after me:
I am IT.
I can change things.
If not me to step up, then who?
If not now, then when?

Self-Assessment: Stepping Up

One of the most critical aspects of harnessing the power of personal responsibility is taking stock of how you are presently showing up. The assessment below is a sort of temperature check on your current level of stepping up. As you respond to each statement, attempt to be as honest as possible with yourself. Imagine that a group of your colleagues, family members, and friends were asked to assess your score on each item based on how you behave day to day. Often by trying to imagine what others observe in us leads to a clearer self-assessment.

In a team setting you could also fill out the survey about yourself and then ask a colleague or two to fill it out as if they were assessing you. You can do the same for them. It can be very instructive to examine any discrepancy between how we see ourselves and how others see us. Often the greatest places of learning come from our blind spots, which are those things that others see about us that we don't see or see less clearly about ourselves. This could be done either in writing or in a one-on-one meeting.

This assessment helps individuals assess whether they have adopted a stepping up attitude. Give each statement below a rating of 1 to 5 on the following scale:

1 Strongly Disagree
2 Disagree
3 Neutral
4 Agree
5 Strongly Agree

_____   I am generally positive when change is happening and like to focus on what I can learn from it.

_____   I generally respond to situations by focusing on what I can do rather than what others need to do.

_____   I think most things that happen to people have been manifested by them.

_____   Most people make their own luck.

_____   I am generally a person who speaks up and challenges things.

_____   I rarely point fingers at others.

_____   I am very open to feedback and seek to understand other people's views more than I defend my own.

_____   I usually think I can influence situations by focusing on the actions I take.

_____   I believe one person can make a big difference.

_____   I don't usually stay focused on my own role but think about how I can make a greater difference.

_____ I think most people underestimate their control or influence on situations.

_____ I rarely focus on what I can't change.

_____ **Add Up Your Total Score**

Assessment Results

54+   Doing well at stepping up; continue to build on it

48–53   Mostly stepping up; identify some key areas for improvement

37–47   Need for improvement; time for a hearty self-inventory

12–36   Definite need to shift your mindset and actions toward stepping up

Self-Assessment: Creating a Culture for Stepping Up

This assessment is meant to help leaders assess whether they have created a culture that is conducive to 100 percent responsibility. In our experience, there is a dance between associates and formal leaders in an organization when it comes to stepping up. We believe that almost all associates want to and have the capacity to step up but that leaders must lead the dance by creating a climate for stepping up behaviors.

There are several ways to use this assessment. You can take this assessment focused on the team that you lead. Think of the questions as asking what kind of climate you have personally created as a leader. As with the self-assessment for stepping up, try to imagine how your team members would score you on each item based on how you show up every day as a leader. Honest self-assessment is critical to growth. If you have areas where you are unsure, why not check in with your team and ask them how they would rate you?

Another way to use this survey is to have your team members or the leadership team of an organization fill it out. If the team members fill it out, then add up the average scores and have a discussion with your team about how you could make improvements. The same can be done if the entire leadership team fills out the survey: aggregate the answers and compare everyone's impressions.

The assessment below is not a precise measurement of a stepping up culture but the foundation for meaningful conversations both among leaders and with their teams.

This assessment helps organizations assess whether they have created a stepping up culture. Give each statement below a rating of 1 to 5 based on the following scale:

1 Strongly Disagree
2 Disagree
3 Neutral
4 Agree
5 Strongly Agree

_____   We give team members a seat at the table to influence decisions that involve them.

_____   Leaders are role models for taking 100 percent responsibility the vast majority of the time.

_____   We recognize well-intentioned actions taken by team members even when they result in failure.

_____   We recognize and reward people for effort and taking responsibility, not merely results.

_____   Leaders are generally open to new ideas and curious when ideas are presented.

_____   Team members feel free to disagree and do not fear the response of those above them.

_____   The organization treats people like adults.

_____   The organization regularly shares information about its performance in an open, transparent manner.

_____ Leaders show positivity and optimism toward and in the midst of change.

_____ Leaders welcome feedback with curiosity as opposed to defensiveness.

_____ Team members have a great deal of latitude to act without asking for permission from leaders.

_____ Team members are encouraged to effect change outside their function and across departments as opposed to "staying in your lane."

_____ **Add Up Your Total Score**

Assessment Results

54+   Great stepping up culture; continue to build on it

48–53   Good culture; identify key areas to improve

37–47   Need for improvement; time for a hearty self-inventory

12–36   Definite need to shift the culture if we want ownership and 100 percent responsibility

What to Do?

- Have all leaders do the assessment
- Create a map of the results
- Have a hearty discussion about your culture and where to focus improvement efforts

Stepping Up for Change

In this book we featured many organizations and individuals who have stepped up to create change. Here is a partial list of websites of those featured in the book:

KIPP, the Knowledge Is Power Program started by Mike Feinberg and Dave Levin, http://www.kipp.org.

BeadforLife in Uganda, helping women and families escape extreme poverty, www.beadforlife.org.

Afroz Shah and the beach cleanup in India. Follow Afroz at https://twitter.com/AfrozShah1.

Global Medic, providing medical relief to the developed world, started by Rahul Singh, www.globalmedic.ca.

United We Can, nonprofit agency founded by Ken Lyotier in Vancouver, www.unitedwecan.ca.

Rex Weyler and the story of the whale campaign, www.rexweyler.com.

Pink Shirt Day, standing up to bullies, www.pinkshirtday .ca.

Howard Behar, author of *It's Not about the Coffee,* www.howardbehar.com.

Marshall Goldsmith, author of the foreword to this book, www.marshallgoldsmith.com.

Discussion Guide

I am so pleased to add a discussion guide to the second edition of *Stepping Up*. Over the past ten years I have heard about many groups forming to study the book together both inside circles of leadership within organizations and among individuals desiring to explore together what it means to take 100 percent responsibility. These reports made it critical to include a guide in the new edition.

The guide is organized by chapter, allowing groups to explore each chapter as they read the book or after everyone has finished the book. I have tried to balance the questions relevant to work, life, and leadership. Therefore, some of the questions will be more appropriate for different groups.

Groups can either read the book in its entirety and select questions to explore or meet after the group has read one particular chapter. I am generally agnostic about the best path except to say that there is some value to digesting concepts more slowly to put them into practice. Most groups will probably find it most practical for everyone to read the entire book and then focus on the questions in a number of discussion meetings.

For leadership or work groups, I think having discussions about each chapter is a good idea while consistently asking, What does this mean for us in our organization/team?

Finally, it's okay to have a discussion group of one. So even solo readers might find this guide of use.

Wishing you well in your hearty discussions.

Chapter 1: The Five Rows of Responsibility

Chapter 1 suggests that taking responsibility changes everything. When we focus on what we can do and what we can influence, we are inherently in a place of power. Izzo uses the metaphor of Five Rows to show that when we focus on what we can do, it creates a "responsibility ripple" that encourages others to act. The story of one small child changing the mood of the rows around him on an airplane becomes a metaphor of what is possible when we begin from a place of exerting whatever power we have in a given situation.

The chapter features a few compelling examples of people who stepped up in their Five Rows, including the founders of KIPP and a woman who stood up to the Mafia in Italy. In both cases, the initial actions of a few individuals created a ripple of others choosing to act. Izzo then brings it home with an everyday example of a couple feuding over the distribution of household chores and what happened when one person stopped focusing on what the other person needed to do and focused instead on himself.

Questions to Explore

- What does it mean to take responsibility for your "five rows" in your life or organization right now?
- Where have you seen the power of the "responsibility ripple" where one person acting propelled others to act?
- Where in your life or organization is there a need for more focus on personal responsibility?

Chapter 2: It's Not My Job, It's Not My Fault

Chapter 2 explores powerful research on why taking personal responsibility is good for our health, happiness, and success. The concept of *locus of control* is explored, whereby we attribute things that happen to us (and to others) to forces either outside ourselves or within ourselves. A person's locus (plural, loci, Latin word for "place" or "location") is conceptualized as internal (a belief that one can control one's own life) or external (a belief that life is controlled by outside factors that one cannot influence or that chance or fate controls one's life). Based on the groundbreaking research of Julian Rotter starting in 1954, we discovered that people who have an internal locus of control, whom the author refers to as "innies," are more successful, happier, more resilient, more admired, and more likely to have successful long-term intimate relationships than those with an external locus of control, whom the author refers to as "outies." The author also shows that over the last several decades, North Americans have become more externally focused with a pervasive culture of victim thinking emerging, whereby people look outside themselves for the source of outcomes.

In every situation, the only thing we have control over is our response to it and what we choose to do. So while external factors do influence us, it makes common sense that those who focus on what they can control are happier and more successful than those who focus on factors outside their control.

Questions to Explore

- Do you think you are generally internally or externally focused? What about your team or organization?
- What external factors are you or your team focused on that you can't change or influence? What *can* you

change or influence, and how might you focus more on those factors?

- What "fixed" mindset do you have about your capacity or capabilities that needs to be challenged?

Chapter 3: I Am Only One Person, or Why People Don't Step Up

Chapter 3 explores why we don't choose to step up and take full responsibility to be agents of change, whether in our personal life or our communal lives. The author conducted a survey to ask that very question with the number one response being "I can't change things/I am only one person." The author challenges us to see why one person matters a great deal. In chapter 1 he discussed the concept of the responsibility ripple. In this chapter, the concept of aggregate influence is explored, which is the idea that while one person acting seems insignificant, the aggregate of many individuals acting is the source of all significant change.

While our action may often feel and seem insignificant, almost all true change has come from individuals choosing to step up in their own way and in their spheres of influence. The author explores the other main reasons people identified as impediments to stepping up: fear of failure, busyness, and waiting for others to act. One by one, each of these reasons is put aside to point us back to choosing to act.

Questions to Explore

- Where have you seen the power of aggregate influence in your work and community?
- What action might you take now in your work, family, or community if you believe it mattered for you to act?

- How do fear of failure and busyness keep you from stepping up to act? How can you neutralize these forces to make way for action?

Chapter 4: Only Naïve People Change the World

Chapter 4 explores one of the key attributes of people who step up to create change: they are naïve enough to believe they can. While this seems elementary in some ways, the belief that it matters if you act is at the heart of creating change. The moment we think "Maybe I can make a change" is the moment that change begins.

Optimism is inherent in stepping up. Most of the people featured in the book had an incredible optimism that their actions would produce results. In this chapter we see a perfect example in Rex Weyler and a group of people who stood up against the commercial whale hunt as well as the cofounders of KIPP.

Questions to Explore

- What role does optimism and the belief in your power to change things have on your willingness to step up?
- One of those interviewed talked about the two voices in our minds as we imagine stepping up. The first tells us we are capable and the second that we are not. How can you counter the voice of pessimism that might keep you from stepping up?
- Where have you seen the power of a belief in the capacity to change things in your life and or organization?

Chapter 5: The 100/0 Principle:
100 Percent Responsibility/Zero Excuses

Chapter 5 focuses on a principle the author has been teaching for over twenty years and is used now by organizations across the globe as a rallying cry for taking responsibility. The 100/0 Principle—the idea of every person taking 100 percent responsibility and making zero excuses—is a game changer. It means every person sees himself or herself as a guardian or caretaker. In a business it means everyone is the guardian of service, morale, efficiency, and quality. In a relationship it means every person is the caretaker of civility, trust, romance, and the health of the relationship. It means zero excuses for not taking the action you are able to take, regardless of what others are or are not doing.

Over the years hundreds of companies and teams around the world have adopted 100/0 based on the author's work. When implementing 100/0 in an organization, it is critical not to use it as a way of blaming and shaming. The best approach is to invite people to explore the power of working with that principle as a guide.

Questions to Explore

- What does it mean for you right now to be 100/0 in your life? In your work? In your organization? How would you act differently if that were your guide?
- What might be the impact on your organization if everyone lived by the 100/0 Principle? Where would it show up in terms of actions and then impact?
- Discuss the story of Joanne Beaton at TELUS. How was she a role model for 100/0? How can leaders be role models for 100/0 in your organization?

Chapter 6: Do Something—Do Anything

Chapter 6 reveals an important feature of stepping up, which is to choose to act even if you aren't sure of the perfect first step. The chapter features two powerful stories, the first about an Irish priest in São Paulo who helped create a movement that transformed one of the most violent slums on earth and the second about a group of frontline employees who started a movement to renew the morale at a large urban hospital.

Both stories show the power of people coming together to simply ask the question, What is one step *we* can take? In the case of the slum, it was to organize a march to the cemetery where many of the victims of violence were buried and then to hold a weekly meeting to ask, What can *we* do to make this community safe? In the case of Mercy Hospital, it was for a group of cross-functional frontline employees to start meeting weekly to simply ask what they could do to respirit a hospital where morale had declined. For each group, the steps needed to achieve their goal did not appear all at once but emerged as they kept asking the question, What can we do? The key here is first to do something and second to focus on what *you* have the power to do without permission.

Questions to Explore

- What does it mean to "Do Something—Do Anything"? Why is it so powerful to take a first action when stepping up?
- Discuss the stories of Jardim Ângela and Mercy Hospital. What are the commonalities between the two stories in terms of how we drive change in systems? What are the key lessons about how we organize together to create change in communities and organizations?

- Why does taking one action often lead us to take further action? What are the perils of waiting for a perfect plan before taking action?

Chapter 7: Always Begin in the Room You Are In

One of the key features of stepping up is to start where you are and to do what you can. While many of the examples in the book appear to be stories of grand impact, almost all of them began with people focusing on something they could do, right in the place where they are. In chapter 7, the author discusses the idea of finding the "possible in the mundane."

If we want to step up to make a larger difference, we need to start by looking around at our current sphere of influence, our five rows, and then ask what we are most capable to do about a situation we care about. Many times those who wound up making a large difference, such as Rahul Singh, who began Global Medic, began by simply asking how they could make a difference right where they were with the skills they already had.

Questions to Explore

- What skills and attributes do you have that best enable you to step up to make a difference?
- As you think about issues you care about at work or in your community, what are you best positioned to do about those issues? What is one step you can take about the issue you care about in your current sphere of opportunity?
- If you or your team were to simply ask, "What action can we do right now," what would that be?

Chapter 8: Leadership Is Not a Position

Chapter 8 focuses on an important element of stepping up, which is that those who make the biggest difference don't let position or a lack thereof get in the way of contributing. The stories in this chapter illustrate the importance of taking the lead to step up to action, whether it is in your job description or whether anyone else has given you the "authority" to lead.

The chapter includes two of the most powerful stories in the book. The first is the story of two Nova Scotia teenagers who stepped up to stand up to a group of bullies in their high school, spawning a global anti-bullying movement, and the second is the backstory behind the origin of the Starbucks Frappuccino, one of the most successful products of our generation. In each case, the people at the center of these incredible stories of stepping up did not have "leader" in their job description. Leadership is a choice to influence, often way beyond and sometimes in spite of, not having an official position to act.

Questions to Explore

- What does it mean to lead beyond your position?
- What keeps you from leading? What mindset did you see in those in the bullying and Starbucks stories and what is the lesson for all of us?
- Where is the greatest opportunity for you to lead right now?

Chapter 9: Stepping Up by Speaking Up

One of the simplest and most profound acts of stepping up is to break the silence. Chapter 9 explores how we can speak up to have more influence. Among other things, the chapter shows that those who speak up in an organization are more likely to be admired, are rated more highly on performance reviews, and are more likely to be promoted. It challenges the assumption that yes-people get ahead, encouraging us instead to constructively speak up to challenge the status quo. Of course, there are risks in speaking up, but we can have a powerful impact by being the ones to break the silence.

The chapter includes a personal story of the author when, as a young minister in the Presbyterian Church, he confronted an elder who routinely told racist jokes. Like the author, many of us feel the pressure to remain silent, fearing going against the crowd. Yet the chapter suggests that these moments when we must choose to speak up or remain silent become defining moments in our lives.

Questions to Explore

- Why is speaking up so important as a way of stepping up? Where have you witnessed the power of speaking up in your life, community, or organization?
- What keeps you from speaking up and breaking the silence? What facilitates a culture of speaking up in an organization?
- Where is there an opportunity for you to speak up constructively now in your life, both personally and at work?

Chapter 10: Stepping Up or Stepping Back: How to Know the Difference

Chapter 10 is the "get real" chapter! One of the most frequent questions people have asked the author in the decade since the book was first published is, What does it look like when I am stepping up or stepping back? The chapter explores five key behaviors that represent stepping up and stepping back action. They are being positive/optimistic versus being negative/pessimistic, having an initiator/action focus versus having a victim/external focus, speaking up/seeking change versus staying quiet/gutting it out, listening/learning versus being closed-minded/defending, and having a head-up/impact focus versus having a head-down/job focus. This chapter invites us to self-evaluate, at each moment, which we are choosing to do: step up or step back. The author also suggests that stepping up is about choosing, moment to moment, to move toward these five behaviors and mindsets.

Questions to Explore

- As you think about the five behaviors, where are you tending to step up and where are you tending to step back? If you were to select only one behavior to work on improving, which would you choose? Where is there an opportunity to practice stepping up right now?
- As you think about your team and your organization, in which of the five areas are people stepping up and in which areas is there a need for a shift?
- How can you stay focused on these behaviors day to day and moment to moment?

Chapter 11: Creating a Company Culture of Stepping Up

Chapter 11 explores how to create a culture for 100 percent responsibility in an organization. Over the last decade the author and his colleagues have worked with several hundred organizations to implement a stepping up culture. In this chapter, the author shares what they have learned alongside some very practical suggestions on what leaders do to create a climate for stepping up.

Three key ideas are shared. The first is to give people a "seat at the table." If we want people to take 100 percent responsibility, we must engage them in the decisions that impact them. The second idea is that getting people to take responsibility requires giving them responsibility. The more we treat people like adults, giving them space to make decisions without asking for permission, the more they will step up to take accountability. The third key idea revolves around giving praise for effort, not only for results. While results matter, if we want people to act outside the box of their defined roles, we must learn to tolerate and even encourage well-intentioned failures as learning opportunities. The chapter is based in part on a survey the author conducted in which people were asked what leaders do that discourages stepping up, with the finding that "leaders making decisions themselves instead of involving others" and "dismissing ideas before exploring them" were the top answers.

Questions to Explore

- As you think about your personal leadership and your organization, how are you doing on the three key elements: giving people a seat at the table, giving them responsibility/authority, and encouraging effort? Where would you and the organization most need to focus to create a 100/0 culture?

- How have you seen these three principles play out in your workplace? What are the lessons from those experiences?
- Reread the story of Don Knauss and the team at Frito-Lay. How does it illustrate the principles in this chapter, and how might they apply in your work situation?

Chapter 12: Who Am I to Step Up?

Chapter 12 focuses on the tendency for each of us to think that we don't have what it takes to step up. Many of the people whom the author interviewed for the book talked about their initial reticence to think that they had what it took to step up and create change. But in each case, these people chose to overcome that hesitance and lean deeply into their capability. This chapter encourages us to make the mental shift from "Who am I to step up?" to "Why not me?"

The chapter includes two powerful stories of people who did not have obvious credentials to step up. The first is about Ken Lyotier, a homeless man who stepped up to help spawn a recycling revolution, and the second is about three women who created a vibrant NGO called BeadforLife. Both cases demonstrate that passion is more important than pedigree and that when we decide to act, helpers inevitably show up. Finally, the author points us again to the two voices that arise when we think about stepping up: Who am I? and Why not me? The choice is ours which voice we heed.

Questions to Explore

- What keeps you from stepping up when you imagine acting? What kinds of mindsets and beliefs undermine your power?
- As you reflect on the two core stories of this chapter—Key Lyotier and the three women who started BeadforLife, what are the lessons you see? How might they apply in your life or organization?
- How and where would you step up right now if you knew you were the right person to do so?

Chapter 13: One Person *Always* Matters

Chapter 13 invites us to step up. Having read the stories of those who stepped up and having learned about the power of personal responsibility, what will we now do? How will we act differently?

The author reminds us that all change comes about because individuals like us choose to step up to act. Real change is not a mystery but the result of each of us in our five rows stepping up to do what we can do. The author shares a personal experience of choosing to step up, even though he was hesitant, and challenges us to choose to be agents of change in this very moment.

Questions to Explore

- The author shared the story about a time in his life when it mattered that he stepped up (along with others) to save green space. When have you had a similar experience? What did you learn?
- How do you want to act and think differently based on what you have learned?
- Where can you most apply the learnings from this book right now in your life and work?

Acknowledgments

Everything we write or say, never mind who we are, is the result of a lifetime of influence whose trail is often hard to discern. I want to thank those who directly contributed to this work but also to recognize those who have contributed to my journey for so many years.

Thanks to the team at Berrett-Koehler for your mission to inspire good in the world. Special thanks to Steve Piersanti at BK, whose gentle guidance helped me let go of the book I should have written to write the book I wanted to write.

Thanks to all who helped craft this manuscript, gave input on titles, and suggested people to interview. Special thanks to Geoff Smart and Jeff VanderWielen, whose comments on the first draft made a significant contribution to this book.

Gratitude to Jeremy Ball, my brother from another mother, who has been as committed to the idea of stepping up as I have been and who has helped shape our work together for over twenty years. You have stepped up yourself in recent years and made a difference in the challenged community of the homeless.

Thanks also to my friends at the Learning Network who are always there to support and challenge me. Special thanks to Marshall Goldsmith for his foreword and to Chris Cappy and Jim Kouzes for their ideas and input. Thanks, Beverly Kaye, for all your encouragement and for the connections you have brought me over the years. You are very special.

Thanks to Devin Hibbard and the entire team at BeadforLife in Uganda along with the amazing women we met while there. The idea for this book really took hold when I saw how you stepped up to make the world a better place.

Thanks to Mark Levy, who gave generously of his time to work on titles and ideas.

To Martin and Farah Perelmuter and their great team at Speaker's Spotlight, I thank you. You have helped get my message out into the world. Thanks for your friendship and hard work.

To my clients, many of whom I interviewed for this book, I say *thank you*. I have always learned as much from you as you have learned from me. Special thanks to TELUS, a company that has been a leader in corporate giving, for producing videos to tell the stories of those who stepped up. Special thanks to Josh Blair and Andrew Turner at TELUS for your friendship and commitment to my work. Bob Peter at the LCBO has stepped up several times to support my work and did so again this time. Thanks to my good friends at Qantas Airlines who put twenty thousand team members through a program to step up. It is a great airline with a great team.

A special thanks to all the people I interviewed whose names and stories are found in these pages. You stepped up, and the world is a better place because of it. I hope I have done your stories justice. You have helped me fulfill that childhood desire to be a journalist.

Thanks to all those who stepped up and helped me at critical times in my life. There are so many of you, but a few stand out: the late Reverend Robert Kelly, whose example of servant leadership shaped my early life; Tony Pontone, who believed in me at a time when I did not believe in myself; Mark Clark and all the professors at Hofstra University who gave me such a good beginning; Trudy Sopp, who first saw my potential in this field and is still a fan (the feeling is mutual); and the late Lynn Rudy, whose torch I still carry.

Thanks to my good friends, new and old, who are far too many to mention by name. To JB, CC (and Ken), and JVW—you guys have gone the distance with me.

Thanks to Janice Halls, my partner in life and love. I waited a lifetime for a friend like you. Even when I thought I should abandon this project, you kept me saying yes. You put up with the ups and downs, always pointing me back up. You are a bright light in the universe, and I'm glad I get to be in your orbit.

My daughter, Lena, who is herself stepping up in a variety of ways—we have been through much together. This life journey would not have been the same without you. I hope you are as proud of this work as I am of you.

Love to my mother, Irene-Parisi Izzo. You kept on trudging through the darkest hours and always kept me doing the same. You left this world for the next one four years ago, but my life continues to be fueled by the fire you lit in me. I think of you every day and miss you beyond belief.

Finally, thanks to all who have ever stepped up to create change whether they succeeded in the moment or not. The world we are creating is being built on your broad shoulders.

Index

Dr. John Izzo

Tom Hawkins Photography

Dr. John Izzo is a bestselling author, a community leader, a journalist, a change agent, executive coach, and one of North America's most sought-after speakers on leadership, corporate culture, personal development, and socially responsible business. Each year he speaks at over one hundred events around the world challenging people to step up to the challenge of leadership.

He is the author of four bestselling books including *Awakening Corporate Soul,* which established him as a pioneer in the movement to create high engagement, socially responsible workplaces. His bestselling book *Values Shift* was ahead of its time when he showed how employee and consumer values were shifting and how businesses would have to adapt to this new set of emerging values, including sustainability and social responsibility.

His book *The Five Secrets You Must Discover Before You Die* is an international bestseller based on his Biography Channel television series in which he interviewed two hundred fifty people ages 60 to 106 asking them to reflect on what they had learned about life.

Over the past twenty years he has spoken to over one million people, taught at two major universities, and helped over six hundred organizations create sustainable cultural change including WestJet, Tim Hortons, Hewlett Packard, TELUS, Applebee's, IBM, Walmart, the Mayo Clinic, and Clorox. His work has been featured by the likes of CNN, CBC, the *Wall Street Journal, Fast Company,* and *Maclean's.*

Izzo holds a bachelor of arts degree in sociology from Hofstra University, a master's in theology from McCormick Theological Seminary, and a doctorate from Kent State University. He has served on the board of several large nonprofit agencies including United We Can, the Canadian Parks and Wilderness Society, and BeadforLife.

Contacting Dr. Izzo

To contact the author or to book a speaking engagement, write to info@drjohnizzo.com.

Visit His Website

Find it at www.drjohnizzo.com.

Follow Him on Twitter

He is @DrJohnIzzo.

Another Book by John Izzo, PhD

The Five Secrets You Must Discover Before You Die

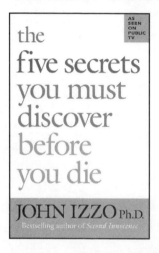

Based on a highly acclaimed public television series, this inspiring book reveals the keys to lasting happiness gleaned from the author's interviews with more than 200 people, ages 60 to 106, who were identified by friends and acquaintances as "the one person they knew who had found happiness and meaning." From town barbers to Holocaust survivors, from aboriginal chiefs to CEOs, they answered questions like, What brought you the greatest joy? What do you wish you had learned sooner? What ultimately mattered and what didn't? Here Izzo shares their stories—funny, moving, and thought-provoking—and the Five Secrets they revealed. This book will make you laugh, move you to tears, and inspire you to discover what matters long before you die.

Paperback, ISBN 978-1-57675-475-7
PDF ebook, ISBN 978-1-57675-551-8
ePub ebook, ISBN 978-1-60509-531-8
Digital audio, ISBN 978-1-5230-8879-9

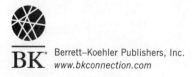

Berrett–Koehler Publishers, Inc.
www.bkconnection.com   **800.929.2929**

Another Book by John Izzo, PhD

The Purpose Revolution
How Leaders Create Engagement and Competitive Advantage in an Age of Social Good

Customers, employees, and investors are no longer satisfied with companies providing good products, good prospects, and good profits—they want them to do some social good too. These "purpose-driven" companies do better on nearly every traditional metric: greater customer loyalty, higher retention, more innovation, and a healthier bottom line. But a nice mission statement and donations to charity won't make your company stand out. Using scores of real-world examples and practical exercises, *The Purpose Revolution* helps leaders find a truly authentic purpose, one that is a natural fit for them and their organization. The authors describe concrete actions leaders can take to ensure that employees own it, customers and recruits connect with it, and every corporate action and activity reflects it.

Print paperback, ISBN 978-1-62656-966-9
PDF ebook, ISBN 978-1-62656-967-6
ePub ebook, ISBN 978-1-62656-968-3
Digital audio, ISBN 978-1-62656-970-6

BK Berrett–Koehler Publishers, Inc.
www.bkconnection.com   **800.929.2929**

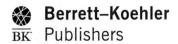

Berrett–Koehler
Publishers

Berrett-Koehler is an independent publisher dedicated to an ambitious mission: *Connecting people and ideas to create a world that works for all.*

Our publications span many formats, including print, digital, audio, and video. We also offer online resources, training, and gatherings. And we will continue expanding our products and services to advance our mission.

We believe that the solutions to the world's problems will come from all of us, working at all levels: in our society, in our organizations, and in our own lives. Our publications and resources offer pathways to creating a more just, equitable, and sustainable society. They help people make their organizations more humane, democratic, diverse, and effective (and we don't think there's any contradiction there). And they guide people in creating positive change in their own lives and aligning their personal practices with their aspirations for a better world.

And we strive to practice what we preach through what we call "The BK Way." At the core of this approach is *stewardship,* a deep sense of responsibility to administer the company for the benefit of all of our stakeholder groups, including authors, customers, employees, investors, service providers, sales partners, and the communities and environment around us. Everything we do is built around stewardship and our other core values of *quality, partnership, inclusion,* and *sustainability.*

This is why Berrett-Koehler is the first book publishing company to be both a B Corporation (a rigorous certification) and a benefit corporation (a for-profit legal status), which together require us to adhere to the highest standards for corporate, social, and environmental performance. And it is why we have instituted many pioneering practices (which you can learn about at www.bkconnection.com), including the Berrett-Koehler Constitution, the Bill of Rights and Responsibilities for BK Authors, and our unique Author Days.

We are grateful to our readers, authors, and other friends who are supporting our mission. We ask you to share with us examples of how BK publications and resources are making a difference in your lives, organizations, and communities at www.bkconnection.com/impact.

Dear reader,

Thank you for picking up this book and welcome to the worldwide BK community! You're joining a special group of people who have come together to create positive change in their lives, organizations, and communities.

What's BK all about?

Our mission is to connect people and ideas to create a world that works for all.

Why? Our communities, organizations, and lives get bogged down by old paradigms of self-interest, exclusion, hierarchy, and privilege. But we believe that can change. That's why we seek the leading experts on these challenges—and share their actionable ideas with you.

A welcome gift

To help you get started, we'd like to offer you a **free copy** of one of our bestselling ebooks:

www.bkconnection.com/welcome

When you claim your **free ebook**, you'll also be subscribed to our blog.

Our freshest insights

Access the best new tools and ideas for leaders at all levels on our blog at ideas.bkconnection.com.

Sincerely,

Your friends at Berrett-Koehler